MAKING YOUR
BRAIN HUM

MAKING YOUR BRAIN HUM

12 WEEKS

TO A SMARTER YOU

JOE BATES, MD

BROWN BOOKS
PUBLISHING GROUP

Making Your Brain Hum: 12 Weeks to a Smarter You

Brown Books Publishing Group
16250 Knoll Trail Drive, Suite 205
Dallas, Texas 75248
www.BrownBooks.com
(972) 381-0009

A New Era in Publishing®

ISBN 978-1-61254-213-3
LCCN 2015955095

Printed in the United States
10 9 8 7 6 5 4 3 2 1

For more information or to contact the author, please go to www.MakingYourBrainHum.com

To My Precious Paula,
Who Survived Guillain-Barré Syndrome
and Fifty Years of Being Married to Me
(Hopefully, many more ahead)

"Knowledge will be pleasant to your soul."

Proverbs 2:10

Contents

Author's Note

The principles outlined in this book should open your eyes and challenge those neurons in your cerebral cortex that have been taking a siesta. Initially, this program was intended to improve cognition for senior citizens, but I was proven wrong in being so limited in scope.

Through continuing my research and personal observations, it became very apparent that the benefits derived from cognitive remediation training (CRT) have a much larger targeted audience. In addition to the elderly, a group to which I proudly belong, the program is being heralded as a seminal intervention to improve the cognitive functioning of patients with chronic mental illness, especially schizophrenia. Additionally, the 2007 *Journal of the American Academy of Psychiatry and the Law* endorsed CRT for "restoring the unrestorable," referring to mental health patients who have criminal charges pending but have been determined to be incompetent to stand trial.

When I was a student at Louisiana State University School of Medicine in the early 1960s, I was taught that dead brain cells were just that—dead! Now research is showing that the human brain is more plastic and regenerative than was ever imagined. The learning process should be endless. Inevitable mental decline after age fifty is a myth. However, the brain can function at peak capacity only when it is used consistently and periodically challenged. Just remember you have to "use it or lose it."

As a psychiatrist and the clinical director of a large Texas mental health facility, I have introduced a program similar to the one in this book to patients with chronic mental illness who, by virtue of their illness with the associated neurotransmitter dysfunction, have regressed in their executive functioning. Though the numbers are small to date, the pre- and post-training data have shown significant improvement across the learning spectrum. Moreover, that advancement has the ability to carry over into other areas, such as self-esteem and socialization.

These also are the same types of exercises I used for personal training before I successfully tested for Mensa, the international high IQ society, just before my seventy-second birthday. If you are embarking on this training to have fun through learning and to maintain your mental agility—bravo! I urge you to continue to develop yourself by pursuing academic endeavors outside your comfort zone. New talents may be discovered along the way that will merge your diversion into a calling.

This book is directed at all those individuals who want to stake a claim on sharpening their mental edge.

Happy learning,

Joe B. Bates, MD, FAPA, FAAP
Diplomate, American Board of Psychiatry and Neurology
Diplomate, American Board of Pediatrics
Member of American Mensa
Tyler, Texas, 2015

Acknowledgments

My appreciation is extended to Brown Books and the superb editing team who guided me through unknown territory. It is also extended to Superintendent Brenda Slaton and Dr. Stephanie Allred at Rusk State Hospital for their support and encouragement when I first proposed this training as a part of the programming for patients.

To my teachers in Homer, Louisiana, public schools and at Louisiana Tech, LSU School of Medicine, and Baylor College of Medicine, I offer my eternal gratitude for instilling the joy of learning. There will always be a special admiration for Mrs. Hessie Watson and Dr. James Moreland from the happy days at Homer High School (Dr. Moreland was later my anatomy professor in med school!), as well as Mrs. Evelyn Hightower and Mrs. Daisy Tinsley, now deceased. Their contributions were immeasurable.

And lastly, to my wife, Paula, who's been there for me through life's ups and downs for over half a century. Honey, you're the greatest!

THE CHALLENGE

"You have to motivate yourself
with challenges; that's how you
know you're still alive."

—Jerry Seinfeld

Chapter 1

Trying to Recall the Brain

The astonishing human brain has been the subject of intrigue and speculation since the dawn of civilization. It can do some amazing things—and humans can do amazing things because of it.

Recent scientific evidence supports the previously unappreciated degree of malleability in the brain's circuitry that can potentially allow for learning throughout life. This neuroplasticity can result in repair that will allow neurons to fire and blood supply to be increased in certain areas of the brain that were never before thought possible . . . a resurgence of "humming," like a well-oiled machine or a fine-tuned car that a driver proudly takes for a spin down the highway. But maintenance is key to the performance, and our brains, likewise, require the same attention.

Data from the Massachusetts Institute of Technology's Department of Neuroscience in June 2014 show that category learning—the type of exercises found in this book—forms connections between two areas of the brain: the prefrontal cortex and the striatum. As these two areas begin to communicate more effectively, the process helps establish a basis for learning and long-term memory formation.

This "humming together" communication has been demonstrated in monkeys during experiments that shifted from rote memorization to learning by categories. This "category learning" resulted in a corresponding shift in the EEG (electroencephalogram) patterns, which reflect the electrical signals generated by the brain. The MIT researchers found that brain waves known as beta bands, produced independently by the prefrontal cortex and the striatum, began to synchronize with each other, suggesting that a communication circuit was forming between the two regions.

Instead of humming, sometimes a person's cognition (the mental processes of thinking, knowing, problem solving, and relating to the environment in a real manner) may fizzle, as in aging and chronic mental illness. Cognitive remediation training (CRT) was developed as an enhancement program to address this critical need through drill and practice of categories that target improvements in the areas of executive functioning: reasoning, memory, speed, concentration, math, and verbal skills. That, in a nutshell, is the premise of this book. Moreover, serendipitous outcomes may include enhancement of other features, such as personality, socialization, self-esteem, and success in work or school.

For those of you in the senior age group, and I include myself, attaining the label of *mental super ager* means we could join that revered legion of elders who in their eighties can compete cognitively with people who are decades younger. Enhancing our chances to become a mental super ager relies on becoming proactive by preserving and strengthening our mental prowess. The process is similar to dusting off the cobwebs of those abilities that we accomplished through educational and skill-training activities as we were growing up and jump-starting them back to life. The adage "You can't teach an old dog new tricks" is archaic and untrue, whether applied to dogs or people.

Remember, a person is never too old to learn. Retirement from work should never mean giving up on learning new information and gaining wisdom.

Instead of fretting about developing dementia, some creative senior citizens and geriatric research centers are focusing on the opposite—enhancing memory and overall mental functioning of the elderly who are fortunate enough to have normal cognitive skills. For example, a recent study called the Advanced Cognitive Training for Independent and Vital Elderly (ACTIVE) involved 2,800 people ages sixty-five and over. The collaborating research centers were located in six US cities. The results were reported in *The Journal of the American Medical Association* and showed dramatic improvement following ten cognitive training sessions. Just ten. Amazing!

Those seniors who did not participate continued to stay the same or showed decline in functioning. Following four sessions of booster training at eleven and thirty-five months after the initial training, the original participants continued to test higher at the five-year follow-up.

The ten-year results of the ongoing study were reported in the January 2014 *Journal of the American Geriatrics Society* with the following conclusion: "Each ACTIVE cognitive intervention resulted in less decline in self-reported IADL [instrumental activities of daily living] compared with the control group. Reasoning and speed, but not memory, training resulted in improved targeted cognitive abilities for 10 years."

More work needs to be done on that memory part! This is the one area in which some degree of slippage is to be expected yet can often be the most concerning to an individual and family members. It is true that occasional lapses in memory are normal in aging adults, but understanding the distinction between normal symptoms and warning signs of Alzheimer's is critical in maintaining cognitive health.

James Russell Lowell, a nineteenth-century poet, stated, "True scholarship consists in knowing not what things exist, but what they mean; it is not memory, but judgment." My conviction is that though our memories may stumble to a certain degree, other areas of mental performance, particularly intellect, insight, and judgment, can be called into play as compensatory mechanisms that contribute to appropriate interaction with the world around us. CRT addresses all of these elements.

Chapter 2

Putting CRT into Action

As clinical director at Rusk State Hospital, a 325-bed Texas state psychiatric facility, I attempted to locate a CRT program for our patients, but there were few to be found that were readily available and easy to implement. I also wanted the syllabus to be one that would lend itself for group or individual study and could be kept for review. Therefore, I wrote my own manual, as presented in this book with minor alterations.

Although the program is in its infancy, seven out of eleven patients in the first basic class performed higher on the RBANS (repeatable battery of neuropsychological assessment) as evidenced by pre- and post-training testing. One patient brought his score up from 72 to 97, an increase of 21 percent. The sub scores for this individual, who elected to continue the training through the advanced programming, were higher than on the pre-test in every domain. The overall average of pre-test scores in this class was 63; the average post-test result was 72, a statistically significant improvement. Overall, 12 out of 22 participants (55 percent) in both basic and advanced groups had higher post-test scores.

At this time, CRT curricula across the country are diverse and unstandardized, combining a variety of computerized programs, mentoring, group processing, and pen and paper activities. To be effective, all of these methods require concomitant psychiatric rehabilitation programming, which includes medication management.

For those patients with mental illness who are involved in fighting daily battles for clarity of thought and stability of mood, CRT should be an important part of the recovery process. An article published in the December 2007 *American Journal of Psychiatry* compared outcomes of CRT for 1,151 patients in twenty-six psychiatric facilities. The results showed 41 percent of the patients made improvements in cognition, 36 percent in psychosocial function, and 28 percent with symptom reduction. The conclusion was that "the effects of cognitive remediation on cognitive performance were remarkably similar across the twenty-six studies . . . despite differences in length and training methods between cognitive remediation programs, inpatient/outpatient setting, patient age, and provision of adjunctive psychiatric rehabilitation. The results indicate that cognitive remediation produced robust improvements in cognitive functioning across a variety of program and patient conditions."

Through my psychiatric practice, I have access to many psychotropic medications that have a dramatic effect on the chemistry of neurotransmitters, resulting in reduction of target symptoms. But at this time there is no medication to increase the cognitive functioning of those patients with severe mental illness, where 98 percent are affected. The changes in functioning induced by CRT point to the fact that cognitive deficits do respond to training and that this improvement affects other important areas of patients' lives.

In my fifty years as a physician, I have been involved in the treatment of certain individuals with mental illness that I consider to be some of the nicest, most endearing people I have ever known, as well as some of the most intelligent. They have included a Pulitzer Prize-winning journalist, a NASA engineer, and myriads of MDs, PhDs, and highly successful professionals. They deserve our best efforts to support and encourage their recovery process.

The only requirements for the program at our facility are (1) a desire to participate in the program, (2) the ability to speak and write English (translation in other languages may be forthcoming), (3) the ability to maintain appropriate behavior in a group setting of six to ten people, (4) lack of a permanent brain injury that would preclude cognitive enhancement, and (5) previous completion of at least a mid-high level of formal education.

Multiple factors, in addition to educational background and motivation, regulate the ability to learn. Some of these can be changed, others not so much.

1. **Time:**
   The clock ticks the same for all of us, though the changes that occur are unique to the individual. Some lucky stiffs age at a slower pace.

2. **Genetics:**
   It's the roll of the gene pool dice, and we can't get a re-roll if we don't like the results. As one of my grandchildren would say, "You git what you git, and you don't pitch a fit." For example, some individuals carry a variation of a gene called ApoE, which has been associated

with an increased risk of developing Alzheimer's. Fortunately, having this gene variation does not always result in the development of the clinical condition.

3. **Toxins:**
    Damage that has occurred may be difficult to correct, but many attacks on the central nervous system can respond to therapeutic intervention through neurogenesis (making new cells).

4. **Physical health:**
    Exercise, restful sleep, good nutrition, and attending to medical needs are critical for optimal mental functioning.

5. **Purpose:**
    Those who have identified and follow a calling are more likely to live up to their intellectual potential.

6. **Love and acceptance:**
    The support of spouses, children, parents, siblings, extended family, and friends cannot be overestimated.

7. **Gratitude:**
    A thankful heart acknowledges the excitement of knowledge and the gift of a quick mind. The mind set of interpreting a glass as half full rather than half empty definitely comes into play.

8. **Mental stimulation:**
    Reading, studying, puzzles, learning a new language, travel, social interaction, music, art, dancing, computer-based brain training games . . . the list is exhaustive. CRT falls into this category.

A passion for life-long learning and the lack of available resources led to the creation of this new curriculum, which is offered to anyone with a desire to improve his or her cognitive functioning and have fun at the same time. There may potentially be a big payoff waiting for all who successfully complete the sessions in this manual—a reawakening of brain power that has been allowed to become dormant through disuse. And that's an exciting opportunity for everyone.

As you complete these exercises, you might even discover new talents you didn't know you had or would have shrugged off as too grand and beyond your reach. Mental decline as we all age is NOT a foregone conclusion. A challenge awaits you as you embark on a journey of optimizing your intellectual potential.

For Further Reading

Amado, Isabelle, and Lloyd I. Sederer. 2013. "What is Cognitive Remediation in Psychiatry and Why Do We Need It?" *Huffington Post,* August 13. www.huffingtonpost.com/isabelle-amado-md-phd/cognitive-remediation_b_3728023.html.

Levi, Linda, Jacob S. Ballon, and Joshua T. Kantrowitz. 2013. "Investigational Treatments for Cognitive Impairment in Schizophrenia." *Current Psychiatry* 12 (September): 38–43.

Massachusetts Institute of Technology. 2014. "Synchronized Brain Waves Enable Rapid Learning." *ScienceDaily*, June 12. www.sciencedaily.com/releases/2014/06/140612121354.htm.

McGurk, Susan R., Elizabeth W. Twamley, David I. Sitzer, Gregory J. McHugo, and Kim T. Mueser. 2007. "A Meta-Analysis of Cognitive Remediation in Schizophrenia." *American Journal of Psychiatry* 164 (December): 1791–1802.

Nasrallah, Henry A., Richard S. E. Keefe, and Daniel C. Javitt. 2014. "Cognitive Deficits and Poor Functional Outcomes in Schizophrenia: Clinical and Neurological Progress." *Supplement to Current Psychiatry* 13 (June): S1–S11.

Rebok, George W., Karlene Ball, Lin T. Guey, Richard N. Jones, Hae-Young Kim, Jonathan W. King, Michael Marsiske et al. 2014. "Ten-Year Effects of the Advanced Cognitive Training for Independent and Vital Elderly Cognitive Training Trial on Cognition and Everyday Functioning in Older Adults." *Journal of the American Geriatrics Society* 62 (January): 16–24.

Tanner, Lindsey. 2013. "Study Seeks Super Agers' Secrets to Brain Health." *Yahoo! News,* August 22. news.yahoo.com/study-seeks-super-agers-secrets-brain-health-071524341.html.

Willis, Sherry L., Sharon L. Tennstedt, Michael Marsiske, Karlene Ball, Jeffrey Elias, Kathy Mann Koepke, John N. Morris et al. 2006. "Long-term Effects of Cognitive Training on Everyday Functional Outcomes in Older Adults." *JAMA* 296 (December): 2805–14.

Wykes, Til, Vyv Huddy, Caroline Cellard, Susan R. McGurk, and Pál Czobor. 2011. "A Meta-Analysis of Cognitive Remediation for Schizophrenia: Methodology and Effect Sizes." *American Journal of Psychiatry* 168 (May): 472–85.

THE TRAINING

"Tell me and I forget,
teach me and I may remember,
involve me and I learn."

—Benjamin Franklin

Getting Started

This cognitive training program contains a series of twelve categories of exercises that should be completed at the rate of one category per week, allowing at least one and a half to two hours on each subject. Study should occur on at least two days per week that are not consecutive. Remember not to rush through. If you have time, supplement the sessions with similar brain games found in printed material or on the Internet.

Undertaking the training with a group of up to ten members can be stimulating because different individuals process solutions in their own unique ways. Seeing how other people think through a problem might give you additional and novel insights. You may want to document your progress and that of your group by arranging pre- and post-training testing with the RBANS or other cognitive testing administered by a psychologist or mental health specialist.

Each category contains an example at the beginning of the section that is similar to the challenges found within the unit, along with an explanation of how the correct answer is derived. Most of the sessions that follow the examples contain two parts: Category A (advanced), which is on a high school/college level, and Category B (basic), which is on an elementary/middle school level. You may find it easier to master the basic questions before attempting the advanced, but you know your ability better than anyone. Answers and explanations are provided for each exercise. No peeking!

The degree of complexity ranges across the spectrum, from easy to moderate in degree of difficulty. Nothing is outlandishly complicated. Many of the items require deductive analytical reasoning to come up with a response. Some of the picture exercises will have alternate solutions, as well as cultural, artistic, or scientific references with which everyone may not be familiar. Thinking outside the box is encouraged.

Supplies needed are pencils, scratch paper, and a timer or stopwatch. In the last two sessions, two electronic games are suggested: *Simon* for memory and *Bop It* for speed. For category 11, memory, having another person read the text as you follow along is suggested.

Ready? OK, step up to the challenge, start the cognitive training, and enjoy. The "humming" is about to begin.

Picture Puzzles Part 1: Odd Man Out

TARGETED SKILLS: pattern recognition, visual learning, reasoning, creativity (looking for non-obvious answers). Play a role in global cognition, everyday activities that are sight related.

EXAMPLE:
In this exercise, there is a series of 4 pictures. You will need to select the one that does not share a common link with the other 3 items. Some problems may have more than one possible correct answer. Some individuals might see patterns that others do not, based on personal experiences. But that's OK, as long as you can justify your categorization. The point of the exercise is to pick up on patterns.

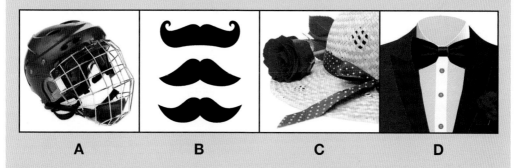

| A | B | C | D |

ANSWER:
C, the woman's hat, since the other items traditionally refer to the male gender. Another possible answer is **B**, moustache, the only non-clothing item.

1.

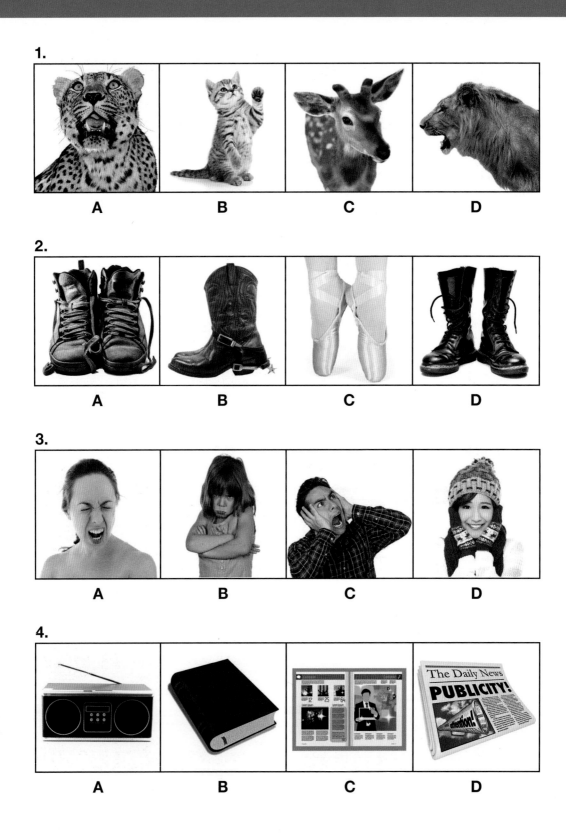

| A | B | C | D |

2.

| A | B | C | D |

3.

| A | B | C | D |

4.

| A | B | C | D |

5.

A   B   C   D

6.

A   B   C   D

7.

A   B   C   D

8.

A   B   C   D

Basic

9.

10.

11.

12.

A   B   C   D

13.

| A | B | C | D |

14.

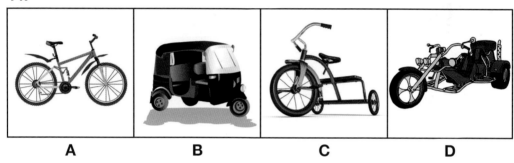

| A | B | C | D |

15.

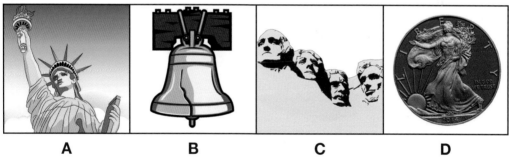

| A | B | C | D |

16.

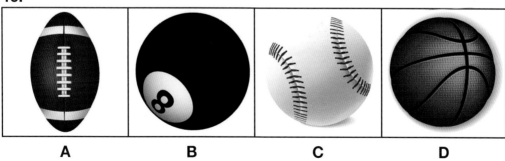

| A | B | C | D |

17.

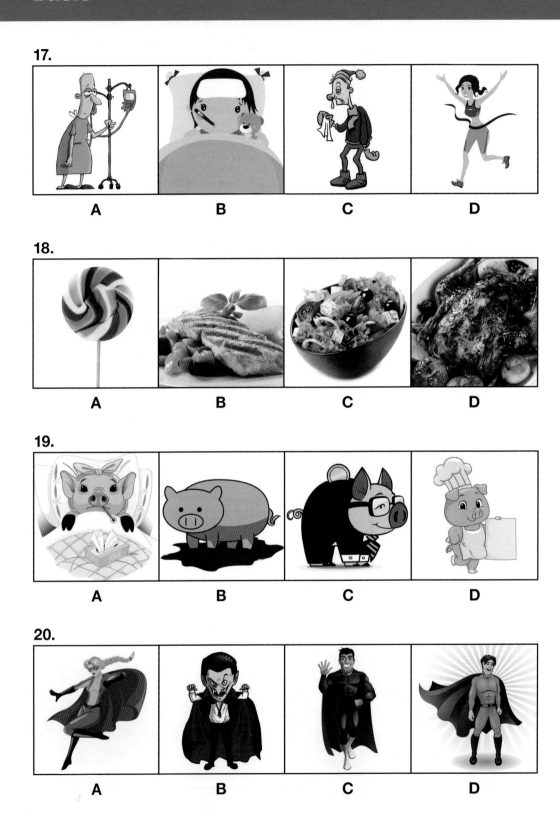

| A | B | C | D |

18.

| A | B | C | D |

19.

| A | B | C | D |

20.

| A | B | C | D |

Answers

1. **C**, fawn. The others are all members of the cat family.

2. **C**, women's ballet slippers. Optional answer **B**, which does not clearly show a *pair* of boots; also, spurs and no laces.

3. **D**, calm emotions. Intense emotions are shown in A, B, and C. The person in D is relaxed and smiling. Alternate answer **C**, the only male in the series.

4. **A**, radio (listening). B, C, and D represent printed material (reading).

5. **D**, rainbow. Tornado, flooding, and airplane crash are disasters.

6. **C**, burglar with gun. The nurse/physician, policeman, and minister are helpers.

7. **A**, skyscraper (man-made). The other pictures show the beauty of nature.

8. **C**, act of aggression. Helping hands and support are represented in the others.

9. **C**, bus. All the other images fly in the air. Alternate answer **B**: the eagle is the only living creature.

10. **D**, happy, feeling victorious. The other people are fearful and worried.

11. **B**, cigarettes. Hygiene products are pictured in A, C, and D.

12. **B**, raccoon. The others are members of the monkey/ape family.

13. **D**, dangerous act of putting hand in alligator's mouth. The others are healthy daily activities.

14. **A**, bicycle. The others have 3 wheels (tricycle).

15. **C**, Mount Rushmore. "Liberty" is the connection. Alternate answer **B**, Liberty Bell, since the other 3 figures all contain faces.

16. **B**, pool ball. The other balls are used for team sports played in a large venue. Alternate answer **A**: the football is not round.

17. **D**, healthy lady. The others all appear to be ill.

18. **A**, candy sucker. Healthy meals are presented in B, C, and D.

19. **B**, drawing of a pig as an animal. The others have taken on human attributes, a term called *anthropomorphism*.

20. **B**, Dracula (bad guy). The other characters are superheroes (good guys). Alternate answer **A**, the only female.

1.

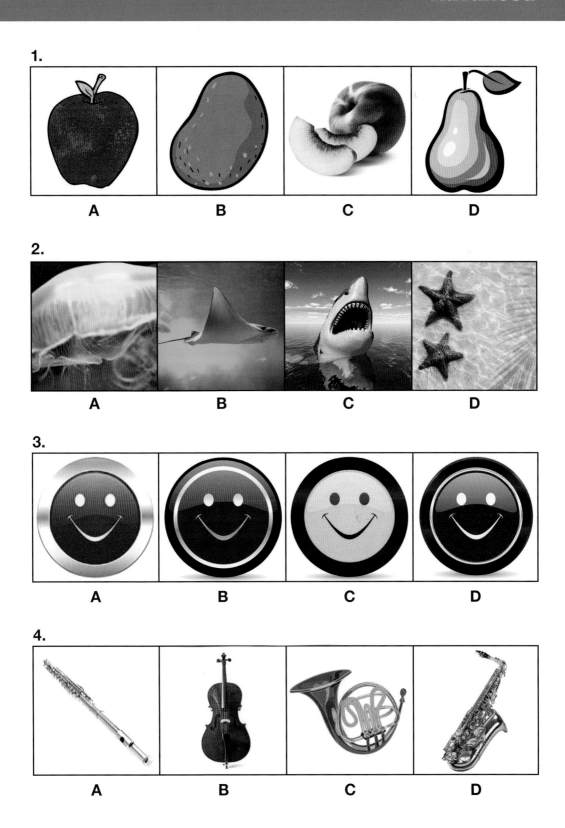

2.

3.

4.

A   B   C   D

5.

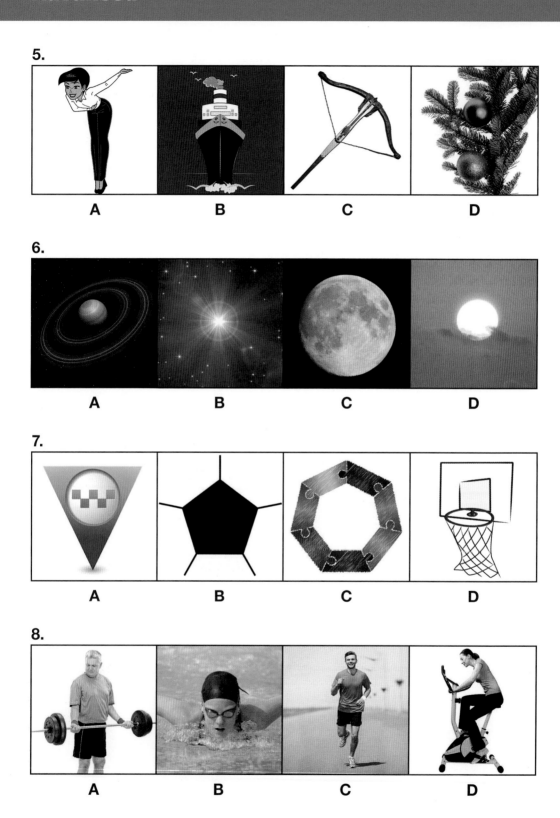

A   B   C   D

6.

A   B   C   D

7.

A   B   C   D

8.

A   B   C   D

9.

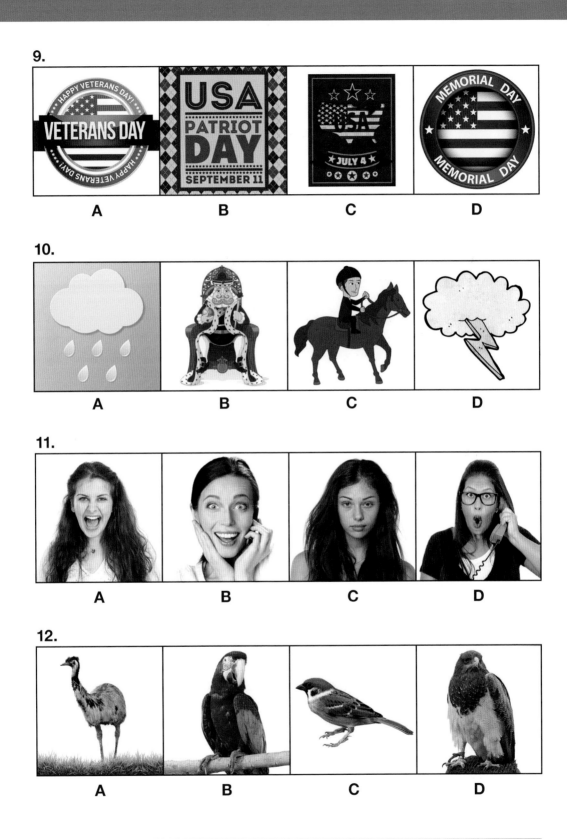

A　　　　　B　　　　　C　　　　　D

10.

A　　　　　B　　　　　C　　　　　D

11.

A　　　　　B　　　　　C　　　　　D

12.

A　　　　　B　　　　　C　　　　　D

13.

A	B	C	D

14.

A	B	C	D

15.

A	B	C	D

16.

A	B	C	D

17.

A   B   C   D

18.

A   B   C   D

19.

A   B   C   D

20.

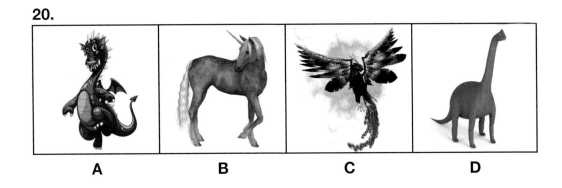

A   B   C   D

Answers

1. **B**, potato. The potato is a vegetable that grows underground. The apple, peach, and pear are fruits that grow on a tree and taste sweet. Alternate answer **C**: the peach has a slice cut out.

2. **D**, starfish. The starfish is harmless. The jellyfish, sting ray, and shark are considered dangerous ocean life.

3. **A**, pink. Pink is not a primary color, as opposed to red, yellow, and blue. Alternate answer **C**, the only image with black eyes and mouth.

4. **B**, violin. The violin is played by hand with a bow. The flute, French horn, and saxophone all require the flow of air to produce sound.

5. **C**, bow. A, B, and D are pronounced *bau*, or alternate answer **D**, bough, different spelling.

6. **A**, Saturn. The planet Saturn with its rings cannot be seen in the sky with the naked eye, unlike the stars, moon, and sun.

7. **D**, basketball backboard. The basketball backboard is in the form of a rectangle, which has 4 sides, an even number. The triangle has 3 sides, the pentagon has 5 sides, and the heptagon has 7 sides, all uneven numbers.

8. **A**, weight lifting. Weight lifting is based on resistance training. Swimming, running, and stationary bike riding are aerobic exercises. Alternate answer **B**, the only exercise in the water.

9. **B**, September 11, Patriot Day, is not a federal holiday.

10. **D**, lightning. The other pictures represent sound-alike words: rain, reign, and rein.

11. **C**, lack of emotion. The girl has a flat affect (lack of emotion). A shows anger, B delight, and D surprise.

12. **A**, emu. The emu is a flightless bird. The parrot, sparrow, and eagle can spread wings and fly. Alternate answer **B**: the macaw is the only one with brightly colored plumage.

13. **D**, firefighter. The firefighter is not part of the military as the soldier (army), pilot (air force), and drill sergeant (marines) are.

14. **A**, ladder. The ladder is not a piece of furniture.

15. **C**, mountain. The mountain vista is a natural wonder. The sculpture, painting, and poetry are humankind's esthetic contribution to the arts.

16. **C**, New York City is not the capital city of the state of New York. Baton Rouge is the capital of Louisiana, Austin is the capital of Texas, and Augusta is the capital of Maine.

17. **A**, penguins. Penguins are found at the South Pole and the southern hemisphere. Polar bears and the aurora borealis are found in the Arctic Circle / North Pole area, identified in image D.

18. **A**, teepee. The teepee is a moveable dwelling, unlike the home, the residence built into the rock, and the rustic cabin.

19. **C**, snakeskin. The claw, eye, and mouth belong to a crocodile.

20. **D**, dinosaur. The dinosaur is a historical animal. The dragon, unicorn, and phoenix are mythical creatures.

Category 2

Word Problems

TARGETED SKILLS: calculation, concentration, reasoning. Help with making change, figuring tip on bill, balancing checkbook, assisting grand-kids with homework.

Problems in this section require basic mathematical skills. Some can be answered with simple mental arithmetic, but you may use a calculator on the harder questions.

EXAMPLE:

As Mr. Brown drives north leaving Apple Town, he identifies 4 possible routes to Banana Village and 3 possible routes from Banana Village continuing north to Coconut City. What is the maximum number of possible routes from Apple Town to Coconut City and return via Banana Village?

ANSWER:

4 x 3 = 12 possible routes from Apple Town to Coconut City and a similar number for the return trip. 12 x 12 = 144 possible routes.

1. Amy visits 3 stores and has $30 to spend. At the first store she spends 1/2 of her money. She then spends $5 at the second store and another $5 at the third store. How much money does she have left?

   A. $10
   B. $5
   C. $15
   D. $20

2. John wants to lose weight by reducing calories by 20% from what he currently eats each day. If he now eats 3,000 calories per day, what will be the new goal for his daily intake of calories?

   A. 2,400 calories
   B. 600 calories
   C. 1,200 calories
   D. 1,800 calories

3. The towns of Alpha, Bravo, and Charlie are in a straight line. The distance from Alpha to Bravo is 10 miles; the distance from Bravo to Charlie is twice as long as from Alpha to Bravo. What is the distance from Alpha to Charlie?

   A. 40 miles
   B. 20 miles
   C. 30 miles
   D. 10 miles

4. Sam drives his truck at an average speed of 60 miles per hour. How long will it take him to go 300 miles and allow time for a half-hour rest stop along the way?

   A. 5 hours
   B. 4 hours and 30 minutes
   C. 3 hours and 30 minutes
   D. 5 hours and 30 minutes

5. John travels to work by bus and train. If his bus ride is 15 minutes, and the train ride is 20 minutes longer than the bus ride, what is the total time for his trip?

   A. 35 minutes
   B. 40 minutes
   C. 50 minutes
   D. 60 minutes

6. A jar of coins worth $10 contains only nickels and dimes. If the dimes make up 1/2 of the value, how many nickels are in the jar?

   A. 50 nickels
   B. 200 nickels
   C. 100 nickels
   D. 80 nickels

7. A pizza sells for $12. If the pizza contains 8 pieces, how much does 1 piece cost?

   A. $1.50
   B. $2.00
   C. $3.00
   D. $0.50

8. On Monday morning, a bakery sold 100 muffins, consisting of straw-berry, vanilla, and chocolate in the ratio of 3:2:5. How many of each flavor were sold?

   A. 20 strawberry, 20 vanilla, and 60 chocolate
   B. 30 strawberry, 30 vanilla, and 40 chocolate
   C. 20 strawberry, 30 vanilla, and 50 chocolate
   D. 30 strawberry, 20 vanilla, and 50 chocolate

9. How many square boxes measuring 1 foot on each side can fit into a larger square box that is 2 feet on each side?

   A. 2
   B. 4
   C. 6
   D. 8

10. A package of candy contains 35 gumdrops, 10 mints, 20 lollipops, and 5 chocolates. What is the percentage of gumdrops in the package?

    A. 35%
    B. 40%
    C. 50%
    D. 70%

11. If a quarter note in music gets 1 count, and a half note gets 2 counts, how many counts does a whole note get?

    A. 1 count
    B. 2 counts
    C. 3 counts
    D. 4 counts

12. One day, Sam and Janet took turns rowing a canoe across a lake. If Janet rowed 10 minutes, and Sam rowed 20 minutes to cover the distance of 450 yards, what was the average speed of the canoe?

    A. 10 miles an hour
    B. 15 yards a minute
    C. 20 feet a second
    D. 30 inches a day

13. Twins Harry and Barry collect stamps. Altogether they have 30. How many stamps belong to Harry if he has twice as many as Barry?

   A. 10
   B. 15
   C. 20
   D. 25

14. Look at the figure below and find the missing numbers for X, Y, and Z if each number in the pyramid is the sum of the 2 numbers immediately below it.

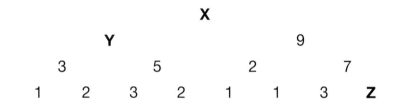

   A. X = 4   Y = 10   Z = 18
   B. X = 21 Y = 8   Z = 5
   C. X = 16 Y = 10   Z = 4
   D. X = 17 Y = 8   Z = 4

15. What number is 20 less than 5 times itself?

   A. 5
   B. 6
   C. 7
   D. 8

16. Ted has $6, Ed has $10, and Fred has $4. If each spends 1/2 of his money at the mall, what is the total amount remaining when they combine their money on the way home?

   A. $5
   B. $10
   C. $15
   D. $20

17. Which is the best bargain?
    A. a 5-ounce can of coffee that costs $3
    B. a 10-ounce can of coffee that costs $6
    C. a pound of coffee (16 ounces) that costs $16
    D. a 20-ounce can of coffee that costs $10

18. What are the missing numbers in the following sequence?

    1 3 6 10 **?** 21 28 **?**

    A. 11 and 30
    B. 15 and 30
    C. 14 and 35
    D. 15 and 36

19. 7 8 3 5 7 2 8 4 3 1 5

    Delete all the numbers that appear more than once in the above list; then multiply the remaining numbers together. What is the answer?

    A. 10
    B. 8
    C. 12
    D. 15

20. On Halloween (October 31), Johnny asks his dad how many days until Christmas. What is the correct answer?

    A. 30 days
    B. 45 days
    C. 55 days
    D. 100 days

Answers

1. **B**, 1/2 of 30 =15, 15 − 5 − 5 = 5.

2. **A**, 20% of 3,000 = 600, 3,000 − 600 = 2,400.

3. **C**, 10 + 20 = 30.

4. **D**, 300/6 = 5, 5 hours for trip, 30 minutes for stop.

5. **C**, 15 + 15 + 20 = 50.

6. **C**, $5 x 20 nickels/dollar = 100.

7. **A**, 12/8 = 1.50.

8. **D**, 30%, 20%, 50% of 100.

9. **D**, 2 x 2 x 2 = 8 boxes.

10. **C**, 35 + 10 + 20 + 5 = 70, 35/70 = 1/2 or 50%.

11. **D**, whole note = 4 quarters or 2 halves.

12. **B**, 450 yd./30 min. = 15 yd./min.

13. **C**, B + 2B = 30, B = 10, 2B (Harry) = 20.

14. **D**, Z + 3 = 7, Z = 4; 3 + 5 = Y (8); 8 + 9 = 17 (X).

15. **A**, 5 x 5 = 25 − 20 = 5.

16. **B**, 6 + 10 + 4 = 20, 1/2 of 20 = 10.

17. **D**, cost per ounce for can A $3.00/5 = $0.60/oz.
                             can B $6.00/10 = $0.60/oz.
                             can C $16.00/16 = $1.00/oz.
                             can D $10.00/20 = $0.50/oz.

18. **D**, the sequence increases by 2, 3, 4, 5, etc.

19. **B**, deleting 7, 8, 3, 5 leaves 2 x 4 x 1 = 8.

20. **C**, 30 days in November + 25 days in December = 55.

1. What number is 1/4 of 1/2 of 24?

   A. 3
   B. 4
   C. 6
   D. 12

2. Find the circumference of a circle whose radius is 5 inches.

   [Hint: circumference of circle = (pi) x (diameter); pi = 3.14]

   A. 6.28 inches
   B. 15.7 meters
   C. 31.4 inches
   D. 40.14 yards

3. If 2 typists can type 2 pages in 2 minutes, how long will it take 8 typists to type 20 pages?

   A. 4 minutes
   B. 5 seconds
   C. 5 minutes
   D. 6 minutes

4. Tom took a history quiz and missed 8 questions out of a total of 40. What is his grade on the test?

   A. 75%
   B. 80%
   C. 20%
   D. 85%

5. If there are 8 tablespoons in 1/2 cup, how many tablespoons are in 6 cups?

   A. 48
   B. 96
   C. 24
   D. 60

6. Bleachers on one side of a soccer field contain 3 rows to accommodate spectators. The first 2 rows measure 15 feet long, and the top row measures 20 feet. Assuming the width occupied by each spectator is 30 inches, how many people can the bleachers hold if completely filled?

   A. 15
   B. 18
   C. 20
   D. 22

7. Sam weighs 1 1/4 times as much as his older brother John weighed at the same age. John currently weighs 150 pounds, which is a 50% increase over his weight at Sam's age. How much does Sam weigh now?

   A. 75 pounds
   B. 100 pounds
   C. 125 pounds
   D. 150 pounds

8. Two trains start heading toward each other over a track that measures 250 miles long. Train A is traveling at a rate of 50 miles an hour. Train B is traveling at a speed of 75 miles per hour. How far from train A's starting position will the trains be when they meet?

   A. 75 miles
   B. 100 miles
   C. 50 miles
   D. 150 miles

9. A rectangular flower bed measures 8 feet by 12 feet. What is the maximum number of rose bushes the bed can hold and meet the following criteria: the plants are no closer together than 4 feet and all plants are at least 2 feet from the border around the bed?

   A. 4
   B. 6
   C. 8
   D. 10

10. John received a college scholarship with the provision that he maintain at least a 3.10 GPA out of a possible 4.0 at the end of each school year. His freshman fall semester grades were: Chemistry, A; Zoology, C; Math, B; History, A; and English, B. Spring semester grades were: Physics, C; Economics, A; French, A; Speech, B; Psychology, B; and Botany, C. Assume that each class counts 3 semester hours, except for chemistry, which counts 4 hours. The grade points per hour are A = 4, B = 3, C = 2. What is his grade point average for the year, and will his scholarship remain in effect?

    [Hint: grade point average is the number of points divided by the number of semester hours.]

    A. 3.02, no
    B. 3.35, yes
    C. 2.99, no
    D. 3.12, yes

11. The ages of sisters Annie, Abigail, Ashley, and Amy total 60 years. Annie is twice as old as Amy. Amy is 6 years younger than Abigail. Abigail is 2 years older than Ashley. What are the ages of the sisters?

	Annie	Abigail	Ashley	Amy
A.	16	14	12	8
B.	20	16	14	10
C.	20	18	15	10
D.	22	17	15	11

12. Bob went to a flea market and took $180 to spend. He spent 1/3 of the total amount on a bookcase. He spent 1/3 of the amount he had left on a pair of binoculars. His last purchase was a painting, which cost 1/2 of the amount he had left after purchasing the binoculars. How much money did he have remaining after all of the purchases?

    A. $40
    B. $25
    C. $60
    D. $80

13. An oil well has been drilled that produces 50 barrels of oil a day. The cost of a barrel of oil is $50. Assuming the landowner receives a 25% royalty, how much is the check for the month of September?

    A. $15,000
    B. $17,500
    C. $16,000
    D. $18,750

14. Most babies are expected to triple their birth weight by 1 year of age. Max weighed 7 pounds at birth but was 33.3% above the expected weight on his first birthday. How much does he weigh?

    A. 18 pounds
    B. 21 pounds
    C. 28 pounds
    D. 30 pounds

15. Twins Ronald and Roland stood back to back and started walking straight ahead in opposite directions. After walking 2 blocks, each turned right and walked another 2 blocks before turning right again and walking another 2 blocks. Then each stopped. How far apart are they?

    A. 2 blocks
    B. 4 blocks
    C. 6 blocks
    D. 8 blocks

16. An airplane travels 300 miles from City A to City B. At City B the airplane takes a right angle turn and travels 400 miles to City C before returning to City A by the shortest route. What is the distance of the third leg of the trip?

    A. 300 miles
    B. 400 miles
    C. 500 miles
    D. 600 miles

17. John runs a lap on the track in 2 minutes. Each lap is 440 yards. How long does it take him to run 2 miles at the same speed?

    (1 mile = 1,760 yards)

    A. 8 minutes
    B. 4 minutes
    C. 14 minutes
    D. 16 minutes

18. How many six-inch square blocks will fit into a container that measures 2 feet wide, 4 feet high, and has a depth of 1 foot?

    A. 16
    B. 32
    C. 64
    D. 128

19. If the annual salary for an employee is $60,000, what is the hourly wage rounded off to the nearest dollar? (Assume forty-hour workweeks.)

A. $29
B. $19
C. $39
D. $49

20. Mary and John started driving across the United States, leaving the Atlantic coast at 8:00 p.m. local time on January 1 and arriving on the Pacific coast at 10:00 a.m. local time on January 5. How long did the trip take?

A. 86 hours
B. 84 hours
C. 88 hours
D. 89 hours

Answers

1. **A**, 1/4 x 1/2 x 24 = 3.

2. **C**, 3.14 x 10 (diameter is twice the radius) = 31.4 inches.

3. **C**, each typist can type 1/2 page per minute. Eight typists can do 4 pages in one minute, so it would take 5 minutes for 20 pages.

4. **B**, 32 correct answers out of 40. 32/40 = 80%.

5. **B**, 8 tablespoons in 1/2 cup, or 16 tablespoons in 1 cup. 16 x 6 = 96.

6. **C**, first 2 rows: 15 feet = 180 inches. Divide by 30 inches per seat = 6 seats on each row, or total of 12. Top row: 20 feet = 240 inches. Divide by 30 = 8 seats. 12 + 8 = 20 seats for all 3 rows.

7. **C**, John weighed 100 pounds at Sam's age. Sam is 25% heavier, or 125 pounds.

8. **B**, Train A will travel 100 miles in 2 hours; Train B will cover 150 miles in 2 hours, which will cover the 250 miles distance. They will meet 100 miles from A's starting point.

9. **B**, total area of the flower bed is found by multiplying 8 x 12 = 96 square feet. Each plant will need 16 square feet to meet the distance requirements (see diagram below). 96 divided by 16 = 6 rose bushes.

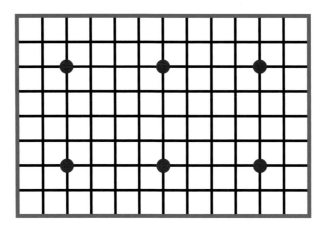

10. **D**, Fall = 16 + 6 + 9 + 12 + 9 = 52/16 hours = 3.25 GPA.
    Spring = 6 + 12 + 12 + 9 + 9 + 6 = 54/18 hours = 3.00 GPA.
    Overall, 106 grade points/34 hours = 3.12 GPA.

11. **B**, the added ages = 60 years with the correct age differences between the sisters.

12. **A**, $180 - $60 (bookcase) = $120 left. Spending 1/3 or $40 on the binoculars = $80 left. The painting cost 1/2 of the 80, or $40. $80 - $40 = $40.

13. **D**, oil pumped from the well will produce revenue of $50 x 50 barrels = $2,500 per day. September has 30 days x $2,500 = $75,000 per month x 0.25 royalty = $18,750.

14. **C**, Max was expected to weigh 21 pounds at age 1. Adding an additional 1/3 (7 pounds) = 28 pounds.

15. **B**, 4 blocks.

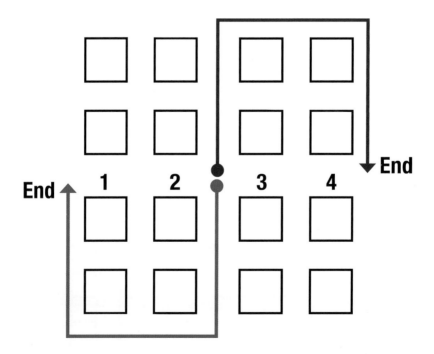

16. **C**, this is the old Pythagorean theorem: $a^2 + b^2 = c^2$
300 squared + 400 squared = 500 squared
where c represents the length of the hypotenuse,
and a and b represent the lengths of the other 2 sides.

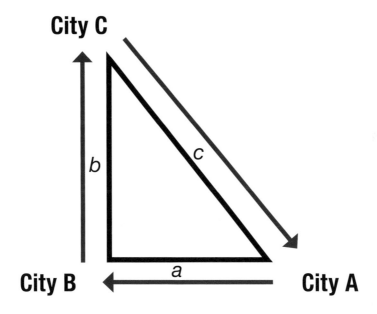

17. **D**, 4 laps of 440 yards equals 1 mile, which would require 8 minutes of running. Two miles = 16 minutes.

18. **C**, the total volume of the container is 2 x 4 x 1 = 8 cubic feet. Each cubic foot of space will hold 8 six-inch blocks. 8 x 8 = 64.

19. **A**, there are 2,080 hours in a work year
(40 hours/wk. x 52 weeks = 2,080). $60,000 divided by 2,080 = $28.84.

20. **D**, Mary and John started in the Eastern Time Zone (Atlantic coast), then the couple headed west, passing through the Central Time Zone, then the Mountain Time Zone, finally arriving in the Pacific Time Zone. Figuring 8 p.m. January 1 until 10 a.m. January 5, it would be 86 hours if the trip had been in one time zone. However, it took an additional 3 hours due to the time zone changes. The arrival time would be 1 p.m. based on Eastern Time.

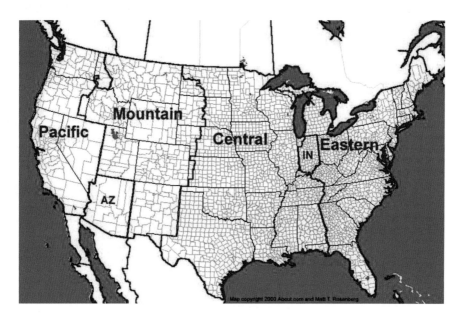

Picture Puzzles Part 2: Matching

TARGETED SKILLS: determining patterns, concentration, visual perception, reasoning. The last four problems in the advanced section also address verbal skills and labeling.

EXAMPLE:
In this exercise there will be an illustration followed by a series of 4 other pictures, one or more of which will have a close relationship with the example. Select the item A–D with strongest common link. Some will have more than one correct answer.

| A | B | C | D |

ANSWER:
B, projector, which goes hand-in-hand with the screen, though all items are movie related.

1.

    A   B   C   D

2.

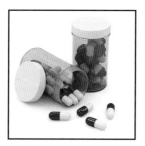

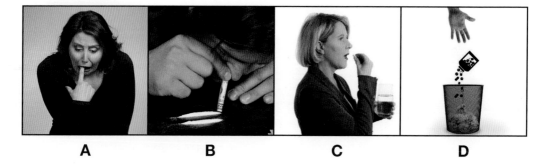

    A   B   C   D

3.

A   B   C   D

4.

A   B   C   D

5.

A B C D

6.

A B C D

7.

A   B   C   D

8.

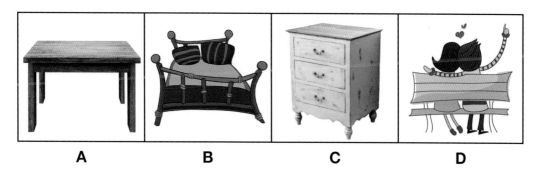

A   B   C   D

9.

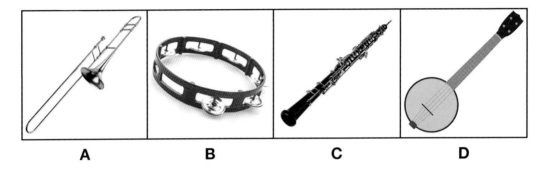

| A | B | C | D |

10.

| A | B | C | D |

11.

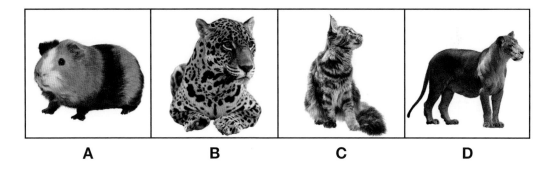

A   B   C   D

12.

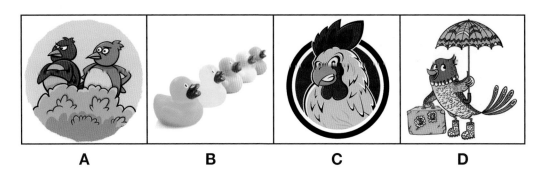

A   B   C   D

13.

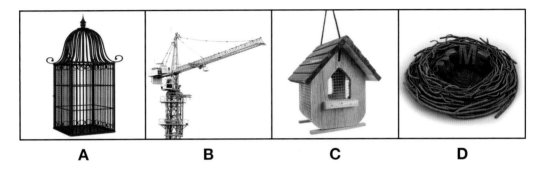

A   B   C   D

In movie theater

14.

A   B   C   D

This happens? Don't . . .

15.

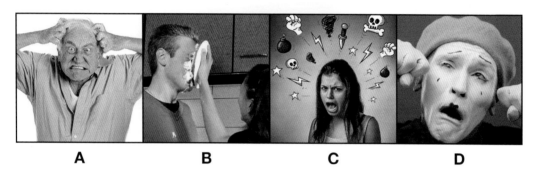

A   B   C   D

16.

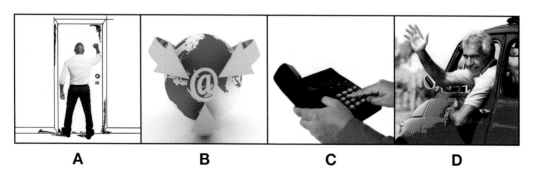

A   B   C   D

Live here? Don't . . .

17.

| A | B | C | D |

HOMONYM

18.

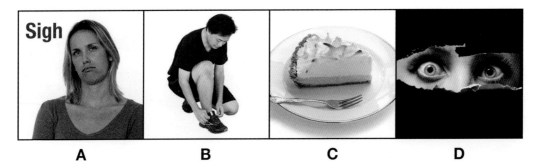

| A | B | C | D |

ANAGRAM: same letters, rearranged

19.

| A | B | C | D |

PROVERB

20.

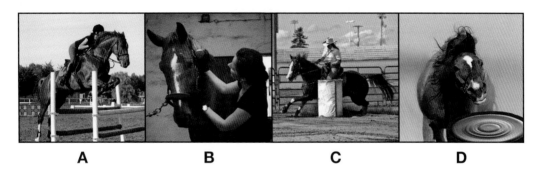

| A | B | C | D |

Answers

1.   **B**, parched man in desert needing water.

2.   **C**, medication . . . pills taken correctly by mouth.

3.   **C**, cupid and love-struck man.

4.   **B**, gasoline and lawnmower.

5.   **D**, school and teacher.

6.   **C**, zoo and ape. The saber-toothed tiger, dodo bird, and wooly mammoth are extinct.

7.   All are possibilities: **A**, both are plants with greenery; **B**, two lips (tulips); **C**, roses (both are flowers); **D**, duckling is also yellow and a sign of spring.

8.   **D**, chair and bench (to sit). Alternate answer **A**, chair (sit at table).

9.   **D**, harp and banjo (string instruments).

10. **A**, shrimp and horseshoe crab (crustaceans).

11. **C**, kitten and domestic cat.

12. **A**, "A bird in the hand is worth two in the bush."

13. **B**, cranes.

14. **B**, smoke in theater and yelling fire.

15. **D**, "Don't cry over spilled milk."

16. **B**, letter and email.

17. **B**, glass house and stone. "People who live in glass houses should not throw stones."

18. **B**, tie (clothing) and tie (laces).

19. **C**, ocean and canoe contain the same letters.

20. **D**, "You can lead a horse to water, but you can't make it drink."

1.

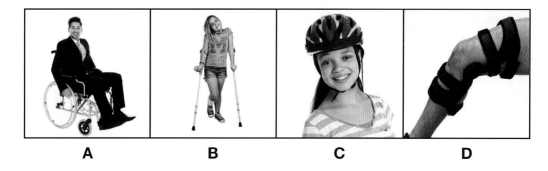

A   B   C   D

2.

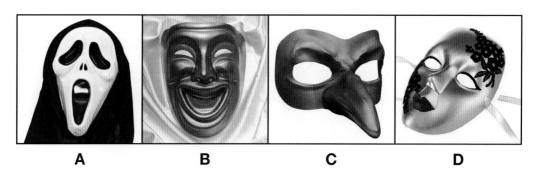

A   B   C   D

3.

| A | B | C | D |

4.

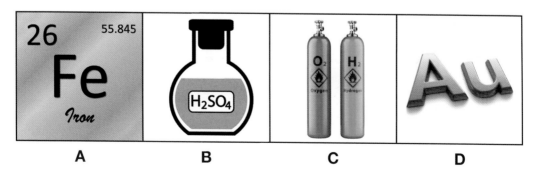

| A | B | C | D |

5.

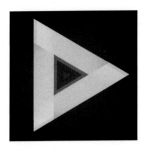

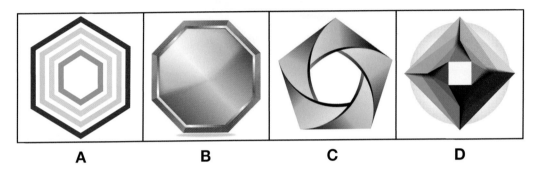

A **B** **C** **D**

6.

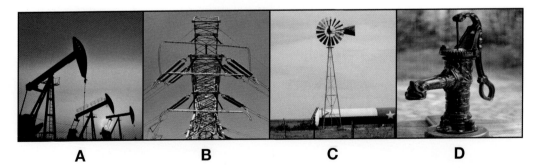

A **B** **C** **D**

Direction?

7.

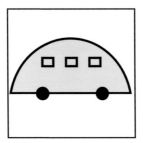

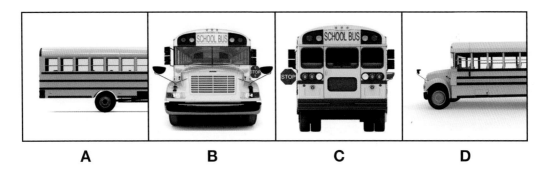

A	B	C	D

8.

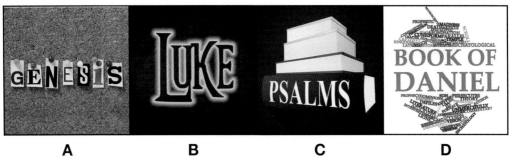

A	B	C	D

9.

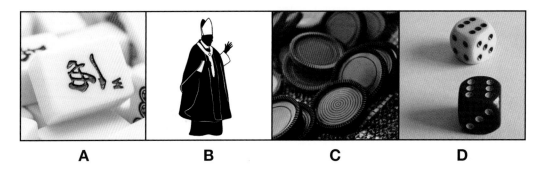

| A | B | C | D |

10.

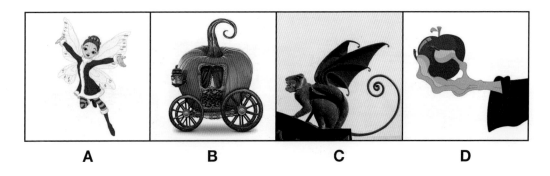

| A | B | C | D |

11.

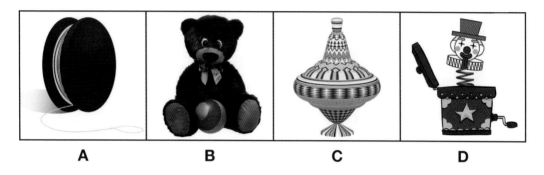

| A | B | C | D |

12.

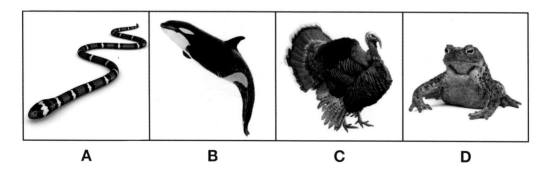

| A | B | C | D |

13.

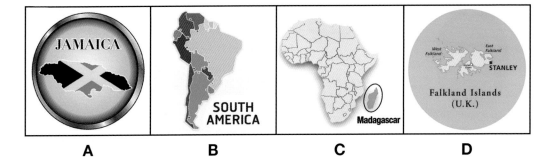

A   B   C   D

HOMOPHONE

14.

A   B   C   D

15.

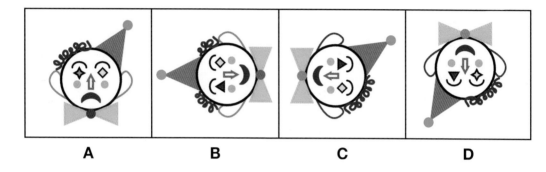

| A | B | C | D |

16.

Spaseeba

| Gracias | Merci | Grazie | Danke |
| A | B | C | D |

HOMOPHONE

17.

A	B	C	D

ANAGRAM

18.

A	B	C	D

HOMOPHONES AND HOMONYMS: Match 1–4 with A–D.

19.

1	2	3	4

A	B	C	D

Get Out of Jail

HOMOPHONES: Match 1–4 with A–D.

20.

1	2	3	4

A	B	C	D

Answers

1. **D**, brace(s).

2. **B**, theater masks (comedy and tragedy).

3. **D**, pine tree and dogwood tree. The others are flowering shrubs: azalea, gardenia, and hydrangea.

4. **B**, NaCl (salt) and H_2SO_4 (sulfuric acid) are chemical compounds. The others are elements (iron, oxygen/nitrogen, and gold).

5. **C**, triangle and pentagram have odd-numbered sides. Others are even-numbered.

6. **A**, oil wells. Also **B** and **C**: all are towers.

7. **D**, both are headed to the left (think where the bus door would be located in the top image).

8. **B**, Jude and Luke are New Testament books. Others are in the Old Testament.

9. **B**, bishop (chess piece). The example is a rook (castle).

10. **C**, from *The Wizard of Oz*, ruby red slippers and flying monkey.

11. **D**, the Russian nesting doll and jack-in-the-box contain hidden figure(s) inside.

12. **B**, camels and whales are large mammals. Alternate answer **A**: camels and snakes are found in the desert.

13. **B**, Australia and South America are continents. Jamaica, Madagascar, and the Falklands are smaller islands.

14. **C**, chorale and corral. Note: glee club is a synonym.

15. **C**, is identical to the lead image.

16. **B**, "Thank you" is reversed between the French/Russian ethnic-dressed characters.

17. **D**, Chile and chili.

18. **B**, sword and words.

19. **A–3**, meet and meat.
    B–4, bail and bale.
    C–1, jazz band and wedding band.
    D–2, eight and ate.

20. **A–4**, kernel of corn / colonel military insignia.
    B–1, mourning symbol / morning.
    C–3, art canvas / canvass (verb).
    D–2, palate (roof of mouth) / artist's palette.

Verbal Challenge

TARGETED SKILLS: vocabulary, reading comprehension, reasoning, concentration, and global cognition.

Verbal training involves selecting the best answer for a variety of word-based problems that involve word usage, definitions, games, and puzzles.

EXAMPLE:

1. Combine 4 of the 10 three-letter bits to produce a word that means "outcome" or "results."

    bar | tid | uen | mak | con | pie | seq | bro | kim | ces

    _____

2. Select the synonym for "obtuse."

    A. loud
    B. intense
    C. dull
    D. silly

3. Select the antonym for "narcissistic."

    A. humble
    B. haughty
    C. hopeful
    D. hateful

4.   Match the phrase "Ew! Eat a ewe!" with the phrase below that shares a common bond. (Palindrome)

    A. Nurses run.
    B. Fish? What fish?
    C. Pale pink pail.
    D. Diggidy dog.

ANSWERS:
1.   con + seq + uen + ces = consequences
2.   **C**, dull
3.   **A**, humble
4.   **A**, palindromes read the same forward and backwards.

SYNONYMS: Identify the word with the same meaning.

1. Clarify

   A. erase
   B. get louder
   C. make clear
   D. confuse

2. Protrude

   A. aim inward
   B. cover up
   C. gaudy
   D. stick out

3. Alternative

   A. funny
   B. fixed
   C. like an altar
   D. choice or option

4. Promotion

   A. downward step
   B. slant sideways
   C. upward position
   D. high school dance

5. Grammar

   A. use of language
   B. use of force
   C. ancestor
   D. type of cracker

6. Punctual

   A. late
   B. on time
   C. delay
   D. blown-out tire

7. Articulate

   A. draw a picture
   B. walk stiffly
   C. speak clearly
   D. stand straight

8. Proverb

   A. wise saying
   B. type of boat
   C. loose garment
   D. farm tool

9. Grievance

   A. gift
   B. complaint
   C. pleasure
   D. thanks

10. Clients' rights

   A. respect and fair treatment
   B. pressure to give in
   C. favoring the rich
   D. changing with whim

WORD GAMES:

11.

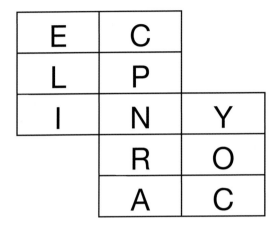

Each six-letter square contains the letters of a word. Both six-letter words are objects that are used on paper. What are the 2 words?

_____   _____

12.

```
T  B  S  W  K      T  T  T
H  L  O  H  I      H  R  H
A  A  D  E  C      E  I  O
```
```
┌──┬──┬──┬──┬──┐   ┌──┬──┬──┐
│  │ H│  │  │ K│   │  │  │ U│
└──┴──┴──┴──┴──┘   └──┴──┴──┘
```

Fill in the boxes to spell a polite response to someone who helps you. Note that short words will be spelled downwards.

13.

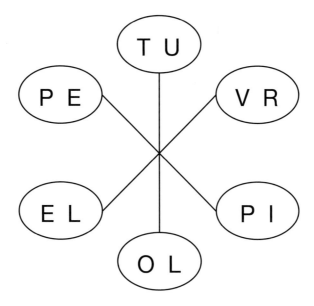

Work clockwise to spell out 2 six-letter words, which are colors that are similar in hue. The letters in each word are consecutive. All letters are used once, and each word starts in a different circle. Each word takes 1 letter only from each circle. What are the 2 words?

_____   _____

14. The clues will lead to a pair of rhyming words.

EXAMPLE: A rabbit that makes you laugh: _Funny_   _Bunny_

A. Obese feline: _____ _____

B. Purple monkey: _____ _____

C. Fortunate webbed-footed fowl: _____ _____

D. Fabric for El Toro: _____ _____

15. THY HYBRID PAPA is an anagram for what saying?

[Hint: think of a special day that you have each year.]

_____   _____

ANTONYMS: Pick the word opposite in meaning.

16. Courteous

    A. rude
    B. helpful
    C. bright
    D. polite

17. Soothe

    A. comfort
    B. relax
    C. agitate
    D. maintain

18. Argumentative

    A. oppositional
    B. defiant
    C. stubborn
    D. cooperative

19. Which 2 words are closest in meaning?

pleasant | unruly | disruptive | strong | recurrent

_____   _____

20. What 2 words are most opposite in meaning?

reliable | inspired | undependable | flowing | previous

_____   _____

BONUS: Combine 3 of the three-letter bits to form a word meaning "sentimental yearning."

tal | fea | hot | san | dro | gia | bam | nos

_____

Answers

1. C

2. D

3. D

4. C

5. A

6. B

7. C

8. A

9. B

10. A

11. Pencil, crayon

12. Thank you

13. Purple, violet

14. A. fat cat
    B. grape ape
    C. lucky ducky
    D. bull wool

15. Happy birthday

16. A

17. C

18. D

19. Unruly, disruptive

20. Reliable, undependable

BONUS ANSWER:
nos + tal + gia = nostalgia

SYNONYMS: Identify the word with the same meaning.

1. Loquacious

   A. silly
   B. flowing
   C. slow-moving
   D. verbose

2. Squib

   A. octopus-like
   B. short witty saying
   C. a scribe's entry
   D. to scrape by

3. Vis-à-vis (two answers)

   A. by way of
   B. in lieu of
   C. face-to-face
   D. in regard to

4. Guileless

   A. dramatic
   B. enigmatic
   C. pensive
   D. sincere

5. Erstwhile

   A. commonplace
   B. current
   C. stunning
   D. bygone

6. Caveat

   A. a warning or caution
   B. resistance to change
   C. neck wear
   D. sharp cliff

7. Taciturn

   A. circuitous
   B. loud
   C. saintly
   D. reserved

8. Magnanimous

   A. overweight
   B. generous
   C. mistaken
   D. clueless

9. Erudite

   A. simplistic
   B. learned
   C. bullying
   D. wandering

10. Picayune

   A. spicy
   B. punishing
   C. foremost
   D. trivial

WORD GAMES:

11.

E	I	T		
L	S	A		
S	E	N	Y	S
		C	A	R
		S	E	E

Each nine-letter rectangle contains the letters of a word. Find the two nine-letter words that are synonyms.

_____   _____

12.

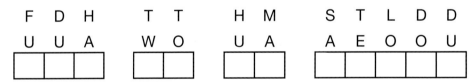

F	D	H		T	T		H	M		S	T	L	D	D
U	U	A		W	O		U	A		A	E	O	O	U

Insert a phrase in the boxes, resulting in a saying that means you don't intend for an incident to happen. There will be 12 three-letter words formed that read downwards.

13.

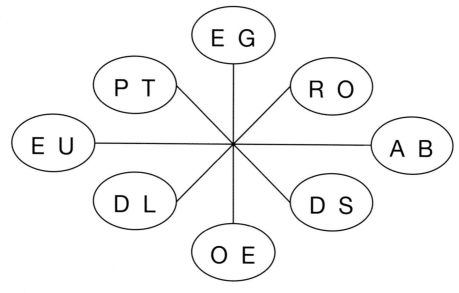

Work clockwise and spell 2 eight-letter words that are antonyms. The letters in each word are consecutive. All letters are used once, and each word starts in a different circle. Each word takes 1 letter only from each circle. What are the 2 words?

_____   _____

14. FUNNY BUNNIES: The clues will lead to a pair of rhyming words.

A. Hip goblin: _____ _____

B. Laconic health professional: _____ _____

C. Unclothed prim & proper person:_____ _____

D. Skinny porcine creature: _____ _____

E. Hauled amphibian (homophone):_____ _____

15. ASHES TWEAK STEAM is an anagram for what phrase that means being in a hurry can cause errors?

_____   _____   _____

ANTONYMS: Identify the word opposite in meaning.

16. Pedestrian

    A. frequent
    B. dull
    C. spectacular
    D. unnecessary

17. Rubicund

    A. round
    B. pale
    C. cubic
    D. healthy

18. Tenable

    A. unbelievable
    B. delicate
    C. spongy
    D. supported

19. Which 2 words are closest in meaning?

strange | formless | hectic | irregular | pallid | angry

_____   _____

20. Which 2 words are most opposite in meaning?

superlative | traumatic | subversive | relaxing | crucial | uncommitted

_____   _____

BONUS: Combine 4 of the 10 three-letter bits to form a word that means "spy" (noun).

con | per | esd | ess | eav | ric | erc | ome | rop | ari

_____

Answers

1. **D**

2. **B**

3. **C** or **D**

4. **D**

5. **D**

6. **A**

7. **D**

8. **B**

9. **B**

10. **D**

11. Essential, necessary

12. Not on my watch

13. Upgraded, obsolete

14. A. cool ghoul
    B. terse nurse
    C. nude prude
    D. twiggy piggy
    E. towed toad

15. Haste makes waste.

16. **C**

17. **B**

18. **A**

19. Formless, irregular

20. Traumatic, relaxing

BONUS ANSWER:
eav + esd + rop + per = eavesdropper

Picture Puzzles Part 3: Series Completion

TARGETED SKILLS: visual perception, picking up on patterns, creativity, reasoning, concentration.

EXAMPLE:

In each challenge in this category, a sequence of 3 pictures is followed by 4 possible solutions. Your task is to select picture A–D that completes the series or shares a common bond.

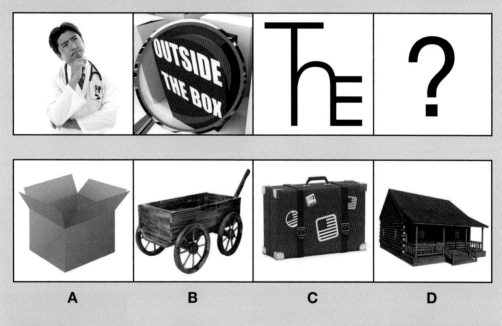

A   B   C   D

ANSWER:

In this puzzle, the correct answer is **A**, completing the proverb "Think outside the box."

1.

A	B	C	D

COMMON SAYING

2.

A	B	C	D

CHILDREN'S GAME

3.

A   B   C   D

COMMON SAYING

4.

A   B   C   D

COMMON SAYING

5.

| A | B | C | D |

COMMON SAYING

6.

| A | B | C | D |

COMMON SAYING

7.

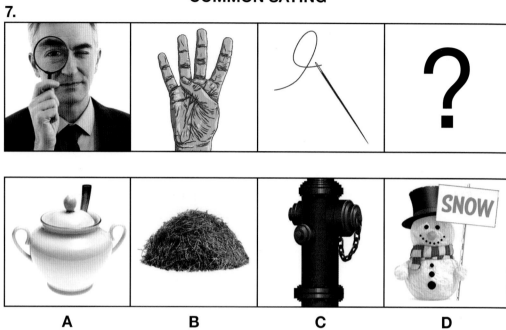

A   **B**   **C**   **D**

8.

A   **B**   **C**   **D**

COMMON SAYING

9.

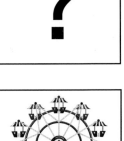

| A | B | C | D |

PROVERB

10.

| A | B | C | D |

PROVERB

11.

A   B   C   D

PROVERB

12.

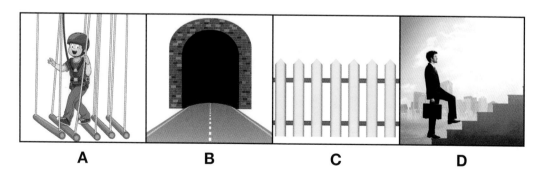

A   B   C   D

13.

A   B   C   D

PROVERB

14.

A   B   C   D

SONG TITLE

15.

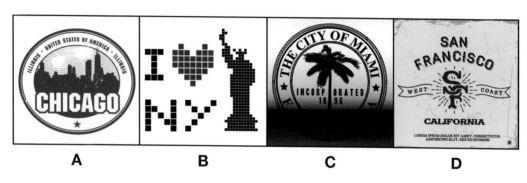

A   B   C   D

16.

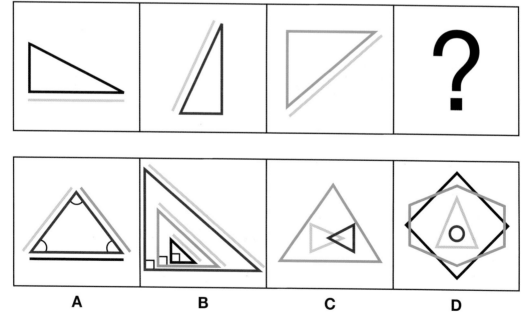

A   B   C   D

CHILDREN'S STORY

17.

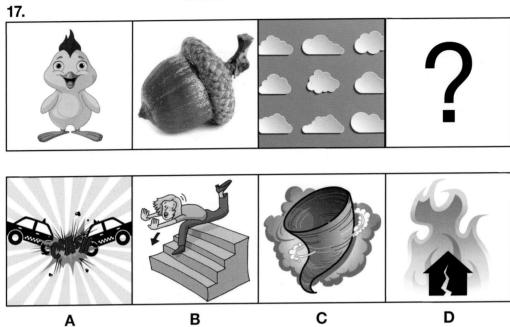

MUSIC

18.

19.

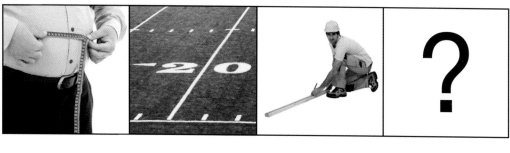

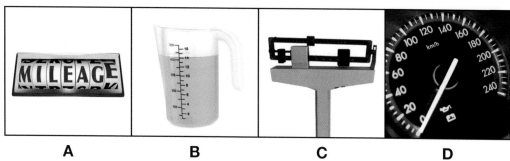

| A | B | C | D |

HOMOPHONES, HOMONYMS, AND MULTIPLE ANSWERS

20.

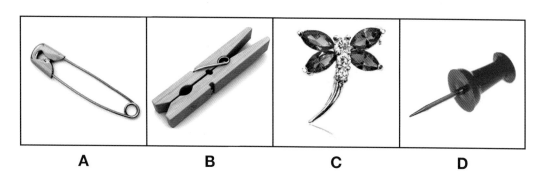

| A | B | C | D |

Answers

1. **B**, the snorkel is for having fun in the water, just like the items in the series. Others are for beach activities.

2. **D**, "That's a horse of a different color."

3. **A**, "Ring around the rosie; pocket full of posies."

4. **D**, "Easy as pie."

5. **B**, "You drive me nuts."

6. **C**, "Penny wise, pound foolish."

7. **B**, "Looking for a needle in a haystack."

8. **B**, baby developmental milestones: infant carrier, crawling, sitting unsupported, taking first step.

9. **B**, "No man is (equals) an island."

10. **D**, "Don't judge a book by its cover."

11. **C**, "An apple a day keeps the doctor away."

12. **C**, "The grass is greener on the other side of the fence."

13. **A**, palace and queen.

14. **B**, "When the cat's away, the mice will play."

15. **D**, "I Left My Heart in San Francisco."

16. **B**, the only right triangles in the groupings (ninety-degree angles).

17. **B**, Chicken Little and "The sky is falling."

18. **C**, do re mi fa, "A long, long way to run."

19. **A**, linear measurements. Others measure volume, weight, and speed.

20. All are correct: variations on "pin" and "pen."

1.

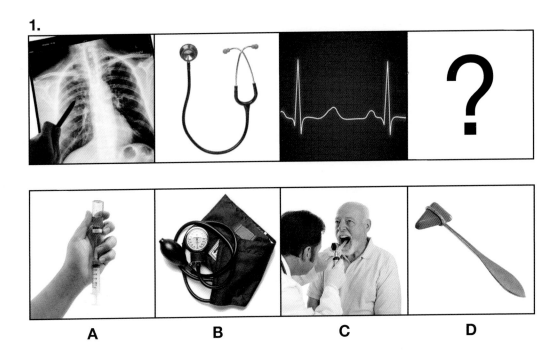

A   **B**   **C**   **D**

2.

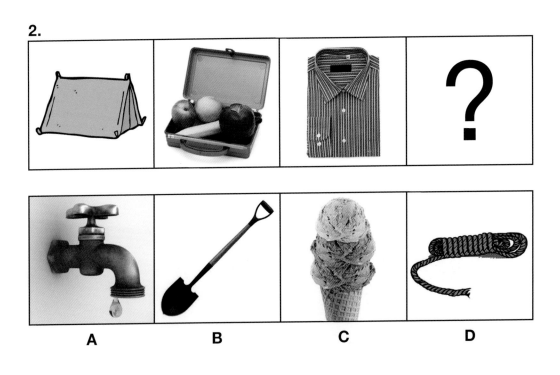

A   **B**   **C**   **D**

3.

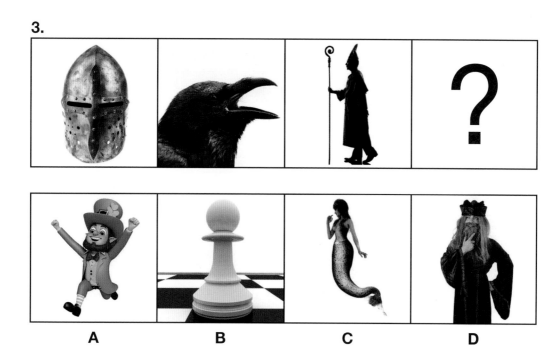

A   B   C   D

4.

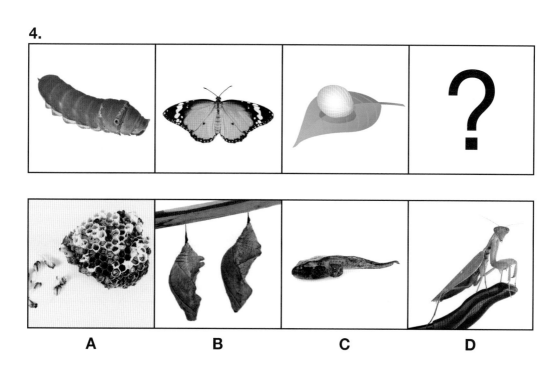

A   B   C   D

5.

A   B   C   D

6.

A   B   C   D

7.

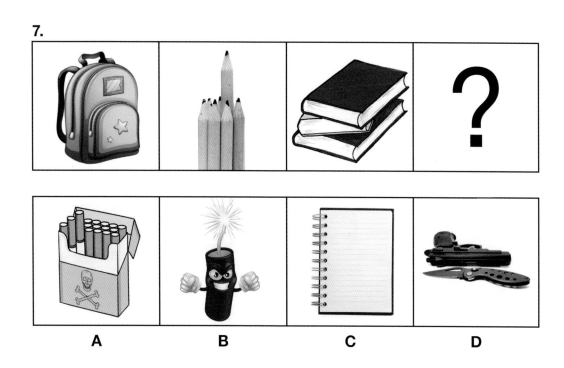

8.

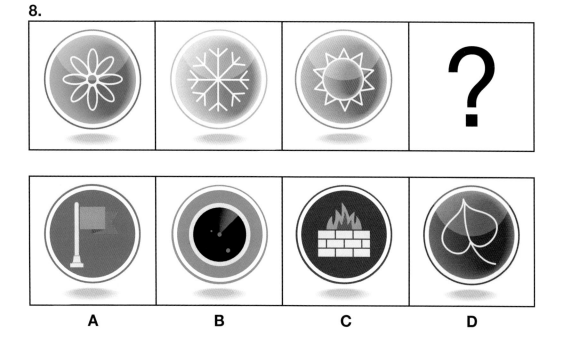

9.

| A | B | C | D |

MORE THAN ONE CORRECT ANSWER

10.

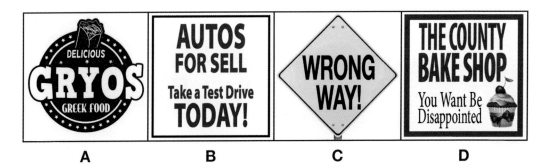

| A | B | C | D |

11.

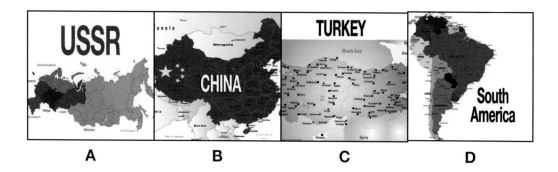

| A | B | C | D |

12.

| A | B | C | D |

COMMON SAYING

13.

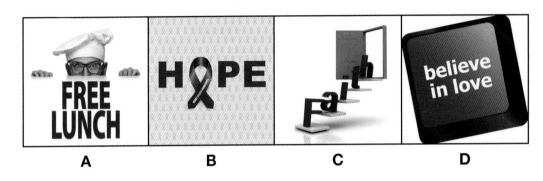

A   B   C   D

PROVERB

14.

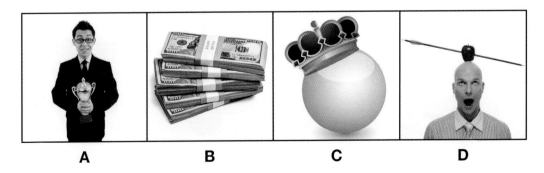

A   B   C   D

PROVERB

15.

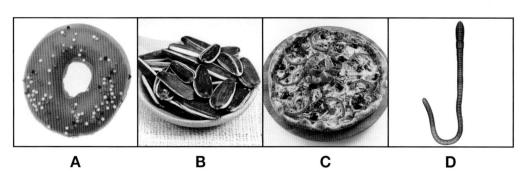

A B C D

16.

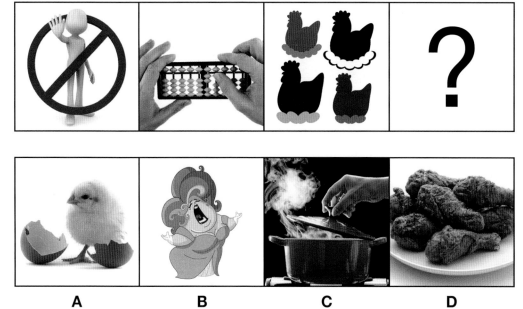

A B C D

17.

A   B   C   D

18.

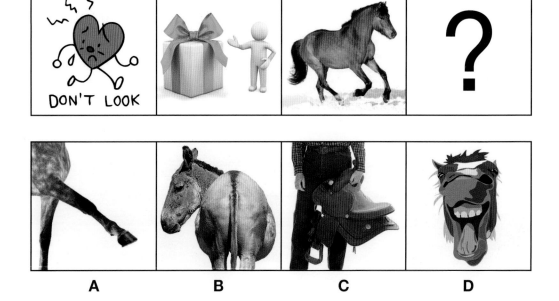

A   B   C   D

PROVERB

19.

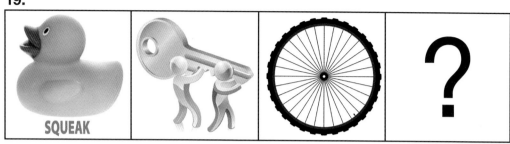

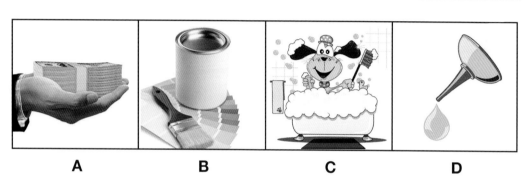

| A | B | C | D |

PROVERB

20.

| A | B | C | D |

Answers

1. **B**, blood pressure cuff helps to evaluate heart function, along with X-ray, EKG, and stethoscope.

2. **A**, water is the stongest answer: essential for life, along with shelter, food, and clothing. **B** (shovel) and **D** (rope) are alternate answers: can also be used in camping.

3. **B**, pawn from chess set. Items above are knight, rook, and bishop, also chess pieces.

4. **B**, butterfly pupa (transition) stage.

5. **D**, singing (howling) can be a coping skill, along with listening to music, and taking a bath, as shown in the top images.

6. **B**, biathalon (cross-country skiing plus rifle shooting) is a winter olympic sport.

7. **C**, notebook is the only item appropriate in a school backpack.

8. **D**, autumn completes the 4 seasons.

9. **C**, judge in courtroom.

10. **A**, **B**, and **D** all have errors of spelling, puncutation, or word usage similar to the top images.

11. **A**, Belarus, Estonia, and Ukraine were once part of the Soviet Union.

12. **B**, music flat sign.

13. **A**, "There's no such thing as a free lunch": common bond with the Easter bunny, gold at the end of the rainbow, and the tooth fairy.

14. **D**, "A fool and his money are soon parted."

15. **D**, "The early bird gets the worm."

16. **A**, "Don't count your chickens before they hatch."

17. **A**, "Too many cooks spoil the broth."

18. **D**, "Don't look a gift horse in the mouth."

19. **D**, "The squeaky wheel gets oiled."

20. **A**, "Love of riches is the root of all evil."

Category 6

Mental Arithmetic Part 1: Coin Counting

TARGETED SKILLS: basic math, speed, concentration, counting money. Help with making change and balancing checkbook.

Problems presented in this category can be solved by simple mental or quick paper calculation.

EXAMPLES:

1. What number is 13 more than 30% of 60 divided by 2/3?

2. What combination of coins equals $5.67?

   A. 2 pennies, 12 nickels, 3 dimes, 9 quarters, 4 half-dollars
   B. 7 pennies, 21 nickels, 3 dimes, 6 quarters, 5 half-dollars
   C. 2 pennies, 22 nickels, 3 dimes, 5 quarters, 6 half-dollars
   D. 2 pennies, 13 nickels, 3 dimes, 4 quarters, 7 half-dollars

ANSWERS:

1. First divide 60 by 2/3 = 60 x 3/2 (remember to invert the fraction for dividing). The answer is 90. Then take 30% of 90 = 27. Add 13 to 27, and the answer is 40.
2. The correct answer is **C**: the sum of this combination of coins is $5.67. Just for practice, determine the value of the other combinations.

For items 1–5, find the combination of US coins that equals the designated amount. You have 15 minutes to answer these 5 questions.

1. $1.65

    A. 5 pennies, 1 nickel, 1 dime, 2 quarters, 2 half-dollars
    B. 0 pennies, 4 nickels, 0 dimes, 4 quarters, 1 half-dollars
    C. 0 pennies, 2 nickels, 1 dime, 2 quarters, 2 half-dollars
    D. 0 pennies, 1 nickel, 1 dime, 0 quarters, 3 half-dollars

2. $2.33

    A. 3 pennies, 3 nickels, 3 dimes, 2 quarters, 3 half-dollars
    B. 3 pennies, 0 nickels, 3 dimes, 0 quarters, 4 half-dollars
    C. 3 pennies, 3 nickels, 4 dimes, 1 quarter, 6 half-dollars
    D. 3 pennies, 1 nickel, 3 dimes, 2 quarters, 3 half-dollars

3. $0.79

    A. 4 pennies, 6 nickels, 1 dime, 0 quarters, 1 half-dollar
    B. 2 pennies, 2 nickels, 3 dimes, 2 quarters, 0 half-dollars
    C. 4 pennies, 0 nickels, 0 dimes, 1 quarter, 1 half-dollar
    D. 9 pennies, 2 nickels, 6 dimes, 1 quarter, 0 half-dollars

4. $3.51

    A. 11 pennies, 2 nickels, 2 dimes, 1 quarter, 6 half-dollars
    B. 1 penny, 1 nickel, 1 dime, 1 quarter, 5 half-dollars
    C. 6 pennies, 4 nickels, 1 dime, 2 quarters, 6 half-dollars
    D. 1 penny, 0 nickels, 0 dimes, 0 quarters, 7 half-dollars

5. $1.15

    A. 5 pennies, 1 nickel, 1 dime, 4 quarters, 1 half-dollar
    B. 0 pennies, 1 nickel, 1 dime, 0 quarters, 2 half-dollars
    C. 5 pennies, 2 nickels, 1 dime, 3 quarters, 2 half-dollars
    D. 0 pennies, 1 nickel, 6 dimes, 1 quarter, 0 half-dollars

Provide the correct responses to questions 6–15. Try to do the math in your head, but the margins may be used if needed for calculation. You have 15 minutes to do this exercise.

6. Multiply 11 by 6 and divide by 3.   Answer_____

7. What is 50% of 90?   Answer_____

8. What is 9 multiplied by 8?   Answer_____

9. What is 497 divided by 7?   Answer_____

10. Add 28 + 27 + 30.   Answer_____

11. What is 9/8 of 80?   Answer_____

12. What is 60% of 250?   Answer_____

13. What is 800 divided by 16?   Answer_____

14. Multiply 48 by 11.   Answer_____

15. What is the square root of 64?   Answer_____

For items 16–25, what is the least number of US coins that will equal the designated amount? Dollar coins are not allowed. You have 15 minutes for this exercise.

16. $4.22   Answer_____

17. $0.38   Answer_____

18. $5.00   Answer_____

19. $2.85   Answer_____

20. $3.46   Answer_____

21. $1.73   Answer_____

22. $0.54   Answer_____

23. $2.07   Answer_____

24. $3.33   Answer_____

25. $0.96   Answer_____

You have 15 minutes to answer problems 26–35.

26. What is 12/16 expressed as a decimal?   Answer_____

27. Divide 42 by 6 and add 13.   Answer_____

28. Subtract 2/5 of 40 from 100.   Answer_____

29. Divide 284 by 4.   Answer_____

30. What is 3/4 times 1/2?   Answer_____

31. What is 2/3 of 6?   Answer_____

32. Add 34 + 23 + 21.   Answer_____

33. Add 3/4 of 12 and 1/2 of 6.   Answer_____

34. Multiply 8 x 10 x 10.   Answer_____

35. Subtract 42 from 65 and add 12.   Answer_____

Answers

1. D

2. B

3. C

4. D

5. B

6. 22

7. 45

8. 72

9. 71

10. 85

11. 90

12. 150

13. 50

14. 528

15. 8

16. **12**: 8 half-dollars, 2 dimes, 2 pennies

17. **5**: 1 quarter, 1 dime, 3 pennies

18. **10**: 10 half-dollars

19. **7**: 5 half-dollars, 1 quarter, 1 dime

20. **10**: 6 half-dollars, 1 quarter, 2 dimes, 1 penny

21. **8**: 3 half-dollars, 2 dimes, 3 pennies

22. **5**: 1 half-dollar, 4 pennies

23. **7**: 4 half-dollars, 1 nickel, 2 pennies

24. **11**: 6 half-dollars, 1 quarter, 1 nickel, 3 pennies

25. **5**: 1 half-dollar, 1 quarter, 2 dimes, 1 penny

26. **0.75**

27. **20**

28. **84**

29. **71**

30. **3/8**

31. **4**

32. **78**

33. **12**

34. **800**

35. **35**

For items 1–5, find the combination of US coins that equals the designated amount. You have 12 minutes to answer these 5 questions.

1. $3.65

    A. 5 pennies, 1 nickel, 3 dimes, 3 quarters, 4 half-dollars
    B. 0 pennies, 4 nickels, 0 dimes, 4 quarters, 5 half-dollars
    C. 0 pennies, 1 nickel, 1 dime, 0 quarters, 7 half-dollars
    D. 0 pennies, 1 nickel, 1 dime, 2 quarters, 3 half-dollars

2. $4.33

    A. 3 pennies, 2 nickels, 2 dimes, 2 quarters, 5 half-dollars
    B. 3 pennies, 1 nickel, 0 dimes, 1 quarter, 8 half-dollars
    C. 3 pennies, 3 nickels, 4 dimes, 1 quarter, 6 half-dollars
    D. 3 pennies, 1 nickel, 3 dimes, 6 quarters, 4 half-dollars

3. $0.89

    A. 4 pennies, 0 nickels, 1 dime, 1 quarter, 1 half-dollar
    B. 2 pennies, 2 nickels, 3 dimes, 2 quarters, 1 half-dollar
    C. 4 pennies, 0 nickels, 0 dimes, 1 quarter, 1 half-dollar
    D. 9 pennies, 2 nickels, 6 dimes, 1 quarter, 0 half-dollars

4. $2.91

    A. 11 pennies, 2 nickels, 2 dimes, 1 quarter, 6 half-dollars
    B. 1 penny,   1 nickel, 1 dime, 1 quarter, 5 half-dollars
    C. 6 pennies, 4 nickels, 1 dime, 2 quarters, 4 half-dollars
    D. 1 penny,   0 nickels, 0 dimes, 0 quarters, 5 half-dollars

5. $2.78

    A. 5 pennies, 1 nickel, 1 dime, 2 quarters, 5 half-dollars
    B. 4 pennies, 1 nickel, 3 dimes, 0 quarters, 2 half-dollars
    C. 3 pennies, 0 nickels, 0 dimes, 1 quarter, 5 half-dollars
    D. 1 penny,   1 nickel, 6 dimes, 1 quarter, 4 half-dollars

Provide the correct responses to questions 6–15. Try to do the math in your head, but scratch paper may be used if needed for calculation. You have 15 minutes to do this exercise.

6. Multiply 22 by 6 and divide by 3.   Answer_____

7. What is 80% of 160?   Answer_____

8. What is 9 multiplied by 12?   Answer_____

9. What is 267 divided by 3?   Answer_____

10. Add 28 + 27 + 37 + 13.   Answer_____

11. What is 9/8 of 200?   Answer_____

12. What is 35% of 150?   Answer_____

13. What is 1,000 divided by 16?   Answer_____

14. Multiply 48 by 12.   Answer_____

15. What is the product of the square
roots of 49 and 121?   Answer_____

For items 16–25, what is the least number of US coins that will equal the designated amount? You have 15 minutes for this exercise.

16. $3.27   Answer_____

17. $1.38   Answer_____

18. $5.10   Answer_____

19. $2.81   Answer_____

20. $4.25   Answer_____

21. 10 pesos (1.00 Mexican peso
equals 0.076 US dollars)   Answer_____

22. 2 pounds (1.00 pound sterling
equals 1.67 US dollars)   Answer_____

23. 3 euros (1.00 euro
equals 1.39 US dollars)   Answer_____

24. 500 yen (1.00 Japanese yen
equals 0.0097 US dollars)   Answer_____

25. 100 rubles (1.00 Russian ruble
equals 0.027 US dollars)   Answer_____

You have 15 minutes to answer problems 26–35.

26. What is 6/9 expressed as a decimal?   Answer_____

27. What is the hypotenuse of a right triangle
whose sides are 4 feet and 3 feet?   Answer_____

28. Add 963 to 471.   Answer_____

29. What is 45% of 120?   Answer_____

30. What is 3/5 times 3/4?   Answer_____

31. What is 3/4 of 36?   Answer_____

32. What is 595 divided by 7?   Answer_____

33. What is 3/8 of 128?   Answer_____

34. Multiply $8 \times 4 \times 10^2$.   Answer_____

35. What is 20% of 135 plus 35?   Answer_____

Answers

1. C

2. B

3. A

4. B

5. C

6. 44

7. 128

8. 108

9. 89

10. 105

11. 225

12. 52.5

13. 62.5

14. 576

15. 77

16. **9**: 6 half-dollars, 1 quarter, 2 pennies

17. **7**: 2 half-dollars, 1 quarter, 1 dime, 3 pennies

18. **11**: 10 half-dollars, 1 dime

19. **8**: 5 half-dollars, 1 quarter, 1 nickel, 1 penny

20. **9**: 8 half-dollars, 1 quarter

21. **3**: half-dollar, 1 quarter, 1 penny = 76 cents

22. **12**: 6 half-dollars, 1 quarter, 1 nickel, 4 pennies = $3.34

23. **12**: 8 half-dollars, 1 dime, 1 nickel, 2 pennies = $4.17

24. **11**: 9 half-dollars, 1 quarters, 1 dime = $4.85

25. **7**: 5 half-dollars, 2 dimes = $2.70

26. **0.67**

27. **5 feet**

28. **1,434**

29. **54**

30. **9/20**

31. **27**

32. **85**

33. **48**

34. **3,200**

35. **62**

Picture Puzzles Part 4: Analogy

Analogy is a cognitive process that involves transferring information or meaning from one subject to another, a type of "mapping" of relationships between objects. Figuring out an analogy is a type of problem solving that brings together cognitive skills such as memory, creativity, reasoning, and decision making.

EXAMPLE:

The concept in this exercise is to determine the ratio, or proportional relation, of the items on each side of the colon (: means "is to"). A question mark, which may appear on either side of the colon between the right 2 figures, represents the item you must select to complete the ratio. In this example, just think what you would expect to see when you look through the instruments on the right of the colons.

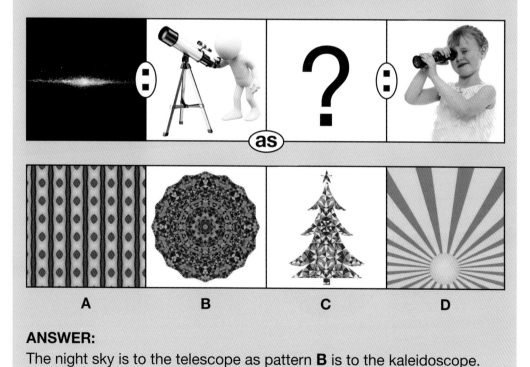

A   B   C   D

ANSWER:
The night sky is to the telescope as pattern **B** is to the kaleidoscope.

1.

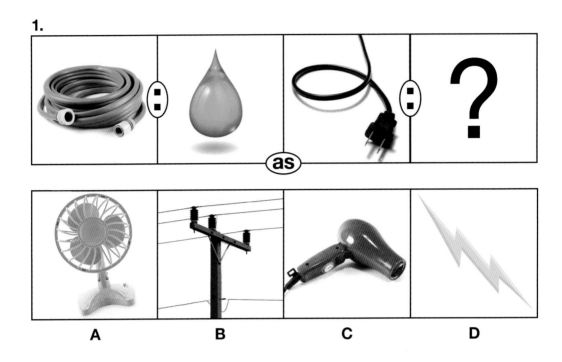

A   B   C   D

2.

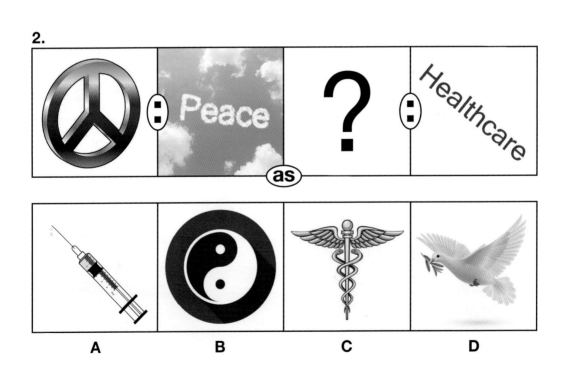

A   B   C   D

3.

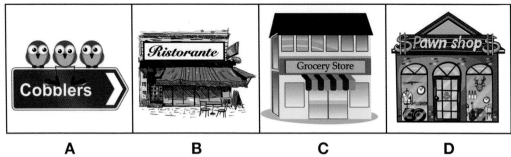

4.

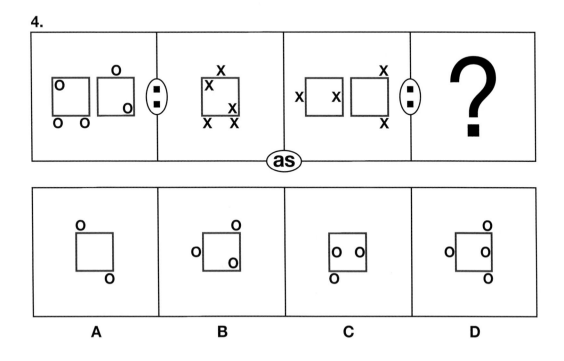

5.

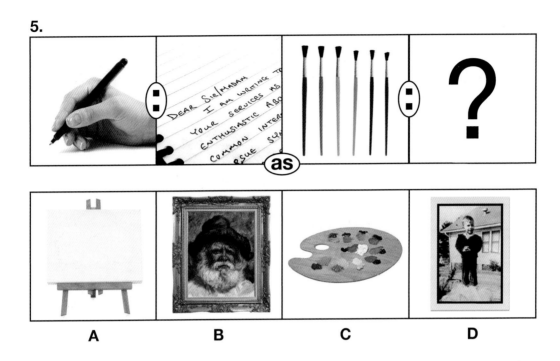

A   B   C   D

6.

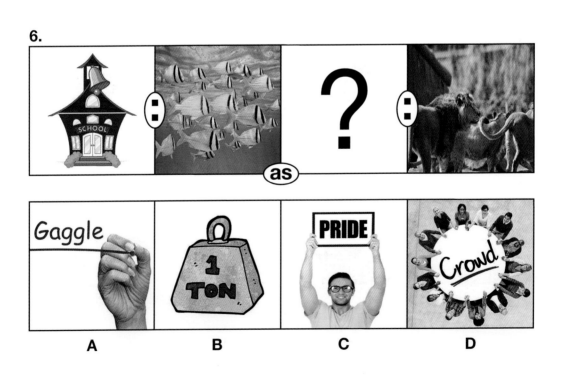

A   B   C   D

7.

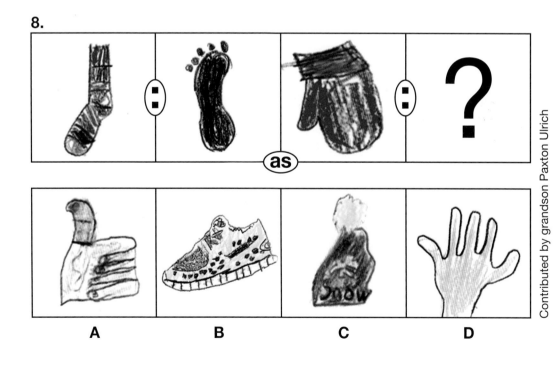

8.

Contributed by grandson Paxton Ulrich

9.

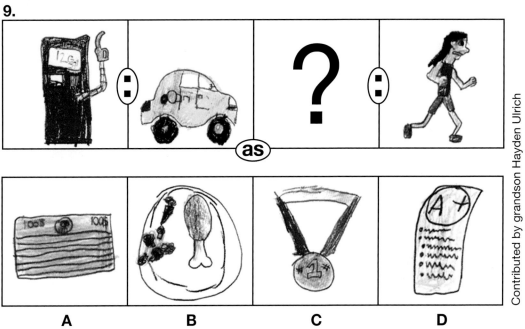

Contributed by grandson Hayden Ulrich

10.

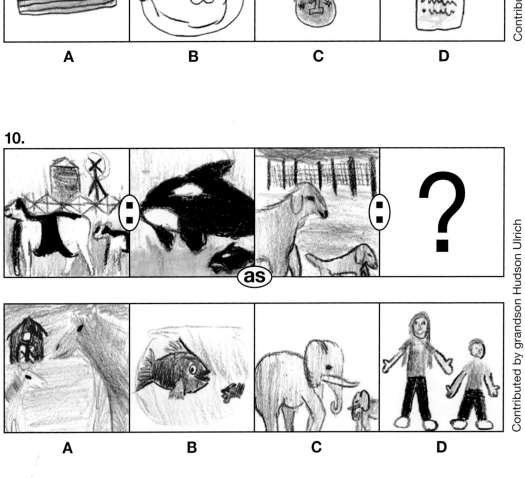

Contributed by grandson Hudson Ulrich

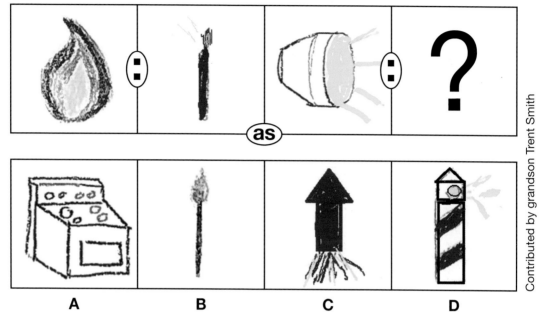

A   B   C   D

MORE THAN ONE CORRECT ANSWER

12.

A   B   C   D

MARRIAGE
License

13.

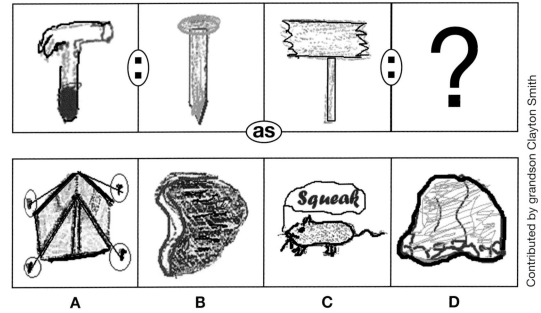

A   B   C   D

Contributed by grandson Clayton Smith

14.

A   B   C   D

Contributed by grandson Kaleb Bates

15.

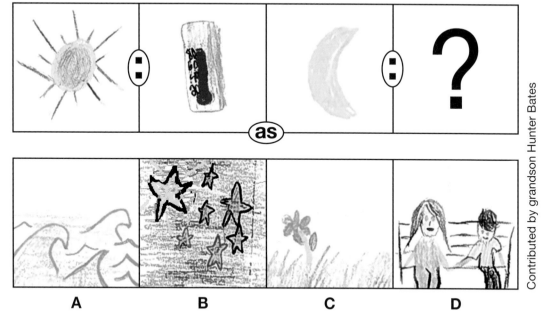

as

A   B   C   D

16.

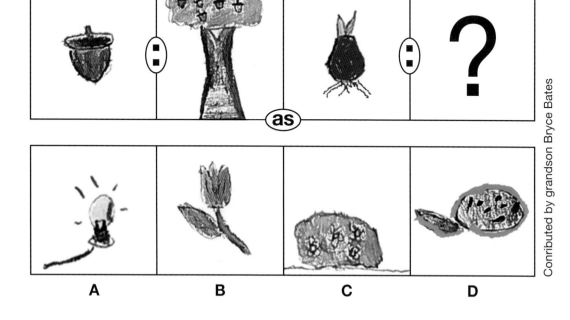

as

A   B   C   D

17.

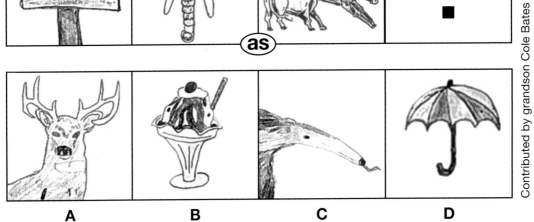

A B C D

Contributed by grandson Cole Bates

18.

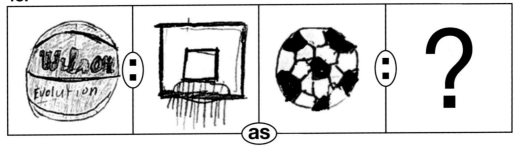

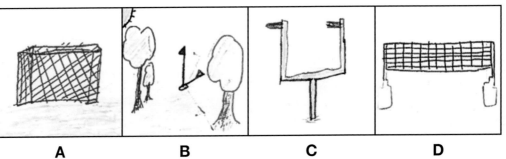

A B C D

Contributed by grandson Travis Bates

MORE THAN ONE CORRECT ANSWER

19.

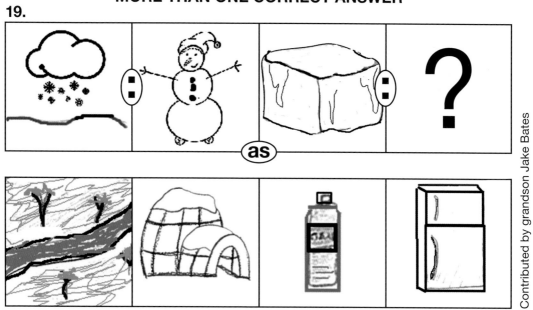

20.

Contributed by grandson Jake Bates

Contributed by grandson Jordan Bates

Answers

1. **D**, hose is to water as cord is to electricity.

2. **C**, peace sign is to peace as caduceus is to healthcare.

3. **B**, mortar/pestle are to pharmacy as fork/knife are to restaurant.

4. **D**, x's are changed to o's and added.

5. **B**, pen is to completed letter as brushes are to completed painting.

6. **C**, school is to fish as pride is to lions.

7. **D**, circle add-ons are reversed, and the horizontal line is carried across the colon.

8. **D**, sock is to foot as mitten is to hand.

9. **B**, gasoline is to car as food (fuel) is to athlete.

10. **D**, dairy cow and calf are to whale cow and calf as nanny goat and kid are to mother and kid.

11. **D**, flame is to candle as beacon is to lighthouse.

12. **A** and **B**, mortar board (graduation cap) is to diploma as bridal veil is to ring and marriage license.

13. **B**, claw hammer is to nail as meat hammer is to steak.

14. **A**, junk mail is to mailbox as spam is to computer.

15. **A**, sun is to thermometer as moon is to waves (tide).

16. **B**, acorn is to tree as bulb is to tulip.

17. **D**, "the panel" is to elephant (anagram = same letters rearranged) as "bull mare" is to umbrella.

18. **A**, basketball is to basketball goal as soccer ball is to soccer goal.

19. **A** and **B**, snow is to snowman as block of ice is to river (melted runoff) and igloo.

20. **C**, reveille is to "get up" as taps is to "lay to rest" (flag-draped coffin).

Category 8

Mental Arithmetic Part 2: Potpourri

This training session is a hodgepodge of problems to improve your sense of numbers. The problems will require reasoning and computation to arrive at solutions, as in the example below.

EXAMPLE:
Look at the straight lines horizontally, vertically, and diagonally in the grid below; determine which one number satisfies all these conditions: it is 3 places away from itself multiplied by 3, 2 places away from itself less 3, 3 places away from itself divided by 2, and 2 places away from itself less 1.

45	9	5	10	44
2	24	14	4	48
11	18	13	27	6
15	3	15	1	27
12	8	7	36	16

ANSWER:
The answer is **4**, which meets all the criteria: 3 places away from 12 (4 x 3), 2 places away from 1 (4 – 3), 3 places away from 2 (4 divided by 2), and 2 places away from 3 (4 – 1).

1.   Sam is 4 years older than Tom. Their combined ages equal 36. How old is each?

   Answer Sam _____   Tom _____

2.   Complete the number sequence: 1, 4, 7, 10, 13, 16, **?, ?**

   Answer _____, _____

3.   The ages of a group of people are as follows: 15, 18, 12, 22, 33. What is the average age?

   Answer _____

4.

33	20	30	29
23	36	26	?

   What number should be in the box with the red question mark? What are the sums of each vertical row and each horizontal row?

   Answers   Red question mark   _____

   Sum of each vertical row   _____

   Sum of each horizontal row   _____

5.   Complete the sequence: 100, 99, 96, 91, 84, 75, 64, **?**

   Answer _____

6.

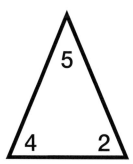 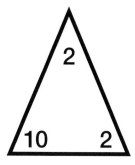 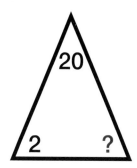

What number should be in the place of the red question mark?

Answer _____

7. What number comes next?   19, 18, 16, 13, 9, **?**

Answer _____

8. Find the 4 consecutive numbers whose sum is 15:

467243913839267845

Answer _____

9. What is 3/4 divided by 3/8?

Answer _____

10.

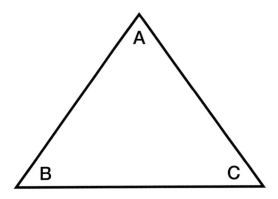

The 3 angles of a triangle (A + B + C) = 180^0. Assume angle A is 70^0 and angles B and C are equal. What is the value for angles B and C?

Answer B = _____ C = _____

11. The ages of Moe and Joe added together is 14. Moe is 3/4 of Joe's age. How old is each?

Answers Moe _____ Joe _____

12. What number is 16 less than 5 times itself?

Answer _____

13. My 3 siblings and I put an equal amount of money into a bank account. When we continue to add to the account so that the total amount is increased by 25%, the sum will equal $250. How much did each contribute at the beginning?

Answer _____

14. Complete the sequence: 2, 5, 11, 23, 47, **?**

Answer _____

15.

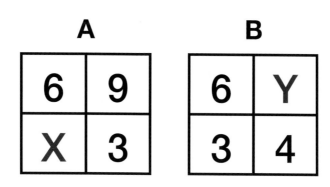

Find the value of X that will make the products of the opposite corners the same number in square **A**. Do the same for Y in square **B**.

Answer X = _____ Y = _____

16. 241:9   342:14   512:7   682:50   732:**?**

Decipher the pattern of the digits on the left side of the colon and their relationship to the number on the right, then supply the answers for **?**.

[Hint: look at 241 as 2-4-1 in the first example.]

Answer _____

17. The average of 3 numbers is 30. If 2 of the numbers are 20 and 40, what is the third number?

Answer _____

18. What number is 3 times 80 divided by 1/2?

Answer _____

19. If A = 1, B = 2, C = 3, and D = 4, solve the following problem:

C x D divided by A + B =

Answer _____

20. 246   810   121   416   182   022

What are the next 3 digits?

[Hint: read the numbers as individual digits 2-4-6, etc.]

Answer _____

Answers

1. Sam is **20**, and Tom is **16**. [T + (T+4) = 36; 2T = 32; T = 16]

2. **19, 22**

3. **20** years (100 divided by 5)

4. **27**. The sum of each vertical row is **56**, and **112** for each horizontal row.

5. **51**

6. **1**. When the numbers in each triangle are multiplied, the product is 40.

7. **4**

8. **1,383**

9. **2** (3/4 x 8/3)

10. **55⁰** (180 – 70 divided by 2)

11. Moe is **6**, and Joe is **8**.

12. **4**

13. **$50**

14. **95**. Each number is multiplied by 2, and then 1 is added.

15. X is **2**; Y is **8**.

16. **23**. The first 2 numbers are multiplied, then the third number is added to get the number on the right side of the ratio sign.

17. **30**

18. **480**

19. **4**

20. **242**. The numbers increase by 2 in a linear fashion.

(Basic algebra may be required for some problems.)

1. Mary is 3 times as old as Betty, but in 4 years, Mary will be only twice as old as Betty. How old is Mary now?

   Answer _____

2. Complete the number sequence: 0, 1, 3, 6, 10, 15, 21, **?, ?**

   Answer _____, _____

3. The ages of a group of people are as follows:

   34, 27, 36, 18, 15, 72, 67, 12, 24, 45

   What percentage of the people in the group are above the average age for the group?

   Answer _____

4.

472	361	589
693	587	142
518	429	?

   What is the missing number?

   A. 627
   B. 981
   C. 498
   D. 367

   Answer _____

5. Complete the number sequence: 3, 6, 12, 21, 33, **?**

Answer _____

6.

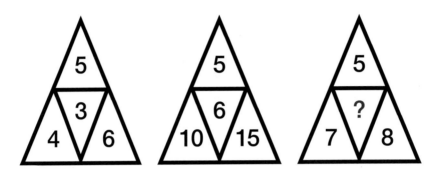

What is the missing number for **?**

Answer _____

7. Complete the number sequence: 2, 7, 22, 67, 202, **?**

Answer _____

8. Find the 5 consecutive numbers in the list below that total 21.

58236394721658234259423

Answer _____

9. What is 3/8 divided by 9/16?

Answer _____

10.

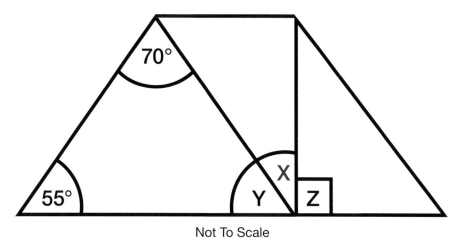

Not To Scale

What is the value of angle **X**?

Answer _____

11. Ted's age plus Ed's age is 27. Ted's age plus Fred's age is 38. Ed's age plus Fred's age is 33. How old are Ted, Ed, and Fred?

Answers   Ted   _____

Ed   _____

Fred   _____

12. What number multiplied by 8 is equal to 63 less than the product?

Answer _____

13. In 4 years' time the combined ages of my 3 siblings and me will equal 208 years. What will the combined ages be in 7 years?

Answer _____

14. Complete the sequence: 5, 6, 7, 8, 10, 12, 14, 20, **?, ?**

Answer _____, _____

15.

2	7
8	6

2	?
7	3

Find the value for **?** so that the products of the 4 figures in each grid are the same.

Answer _____

16. 425:13   643:27   784:60   378:29   579:**?**

Find the value of **?** by deciphering the code for the relationship between the digits on the left side of the colon to the number on the right.

Answer _____

17. The average of 3 numbers is 29. The average of 2 of these numbers is 41. What is the third number?

Answer _____

18. What number is 3 times 60 divided by 1/4?

Answer _____

19. If A = 3, B = 4, C = 5, and D = 6, calculate the following:

(A X C) + (B X D) divided by (A X B) + (D − C)

Answer _____

20. 369, 121, 518, 212, 427, 303, **?**

What three-digit number comes next?

[Hint: look at the numbers as digits.]

Answer _____

Advanced

Answers

1. Mary is **12** now. In 4 years, Mary will be 16. Betty is 4 and will be 8 in 4 years.

2. **28**, **36**. Increases are by 1, 2, 3, 4, etc.

3. **40%**. Average age is 35.

4. **D**. Each row horizontally and vertically contains the digits 1–9.

5. **48**. Each number increases by multiple of 3 (+3, +6, +9, +12, +15).

6. **4**. The numbers at the angles are added and divided by 5 (number at the apex of the triangle).

7. **607**. Each successive number is multiplied by 3, then +1.

8. **72165** = 21

9. **2/3**. (3/8 x 16/9)

10. **35⁰**. The 3 angles of a triangle = 180^0. Angle Z is a right angle (90^0); so angles x + y also = 90^0. To find angle y, $180 - 55 - 70 = 55^0$. Therefore, 90 (angles x + y) − 55 (angle y) = 35^0 (angle x).

11. Ted is **16**, Ed is **11**, Fred is **22**.
    ED   FRED
    (27 - T) + (38 - T) = 33 ⟶ 65 - 2T = 33 ⟶ 32 = 2T ⟶ T (Ted) = 16

12. **9**. (8 x 9 = 72; 72 – 9 = 63)

13. **220**. 208 – (4 x 4) = 192
              192 + (7 x 4) = 220

14. **19**, **36**. There are 2 sequences: the first digit (5) increases in a linear progression every other number by 2, 3, 4, 5; the second digit (6) increases every other number as a multiple of 2 (2, 4, 8, 16).

15. **16**

16. **44**. (5 x 7 + 9)

17. **5**. (A + B + C) x 3 = 29 x 3 = 87; (A + B) x 2 = 41 x 2 = 82;
     C = 87 − 82 = 5.

18. **720**

19. **3**

20. **336** (continuous progression by 3: 3-6-9-12-15-18, etc.)

Category 9

Visual/Spatial

For most people, this is a difficult category. The exercises will require you to think in 3 dimensions and see "hidden" areas behind folds or on the other sides of figures. The example below is one of my favorites and one that I learned at an early age. Make sure you follow the folds exactly, and it never fails!

EXAMPLE:

Fold a rectangular sheet of paper in the following manner:

1. Right corner **A** to left margin **B**.
2. Left corner **C** to right margin **D**.

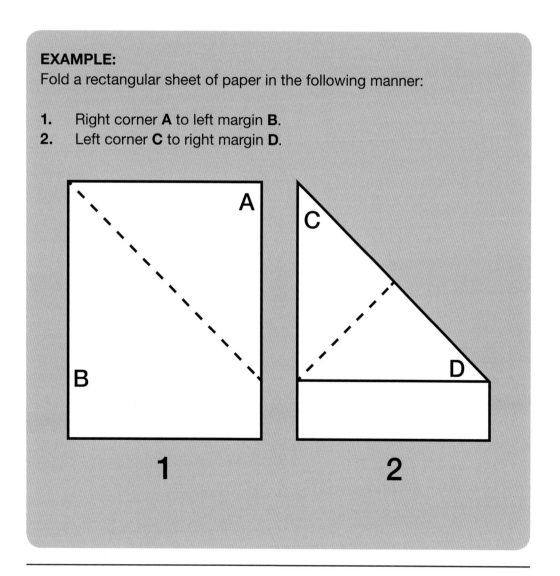

3. Center tip **E** downward, creasing across the middle of the sheet

4. Left side **F** to right side **G**

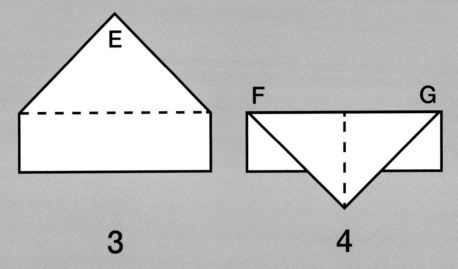

5. Make a downward vertical cut 1 inch from the folded edge and discard the right portion.

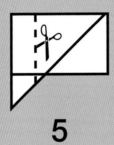

5

When the creased left side of the paper is unfolded, the result will be a

A. square
B. triangle
C. star
D. cross

ANSWER:
D, cross. Did you get it?

1. Select the line that is most closely positioned at the same angle as the example below.

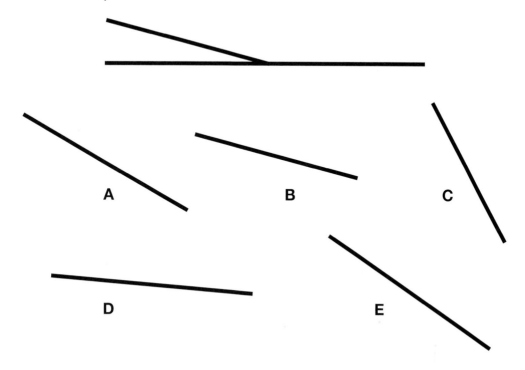

2. Which figure comes next?

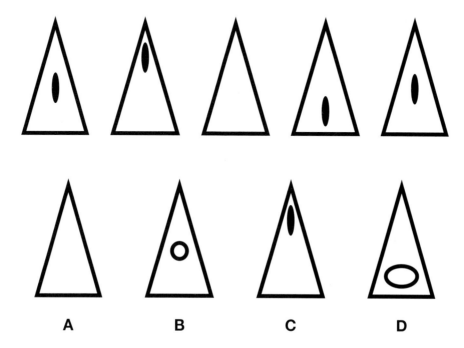

3. Which is the odd one out?

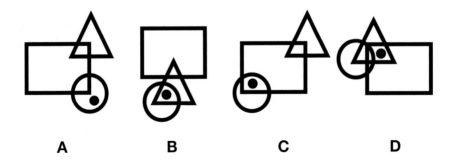

A   B   C   D

4. Solve:

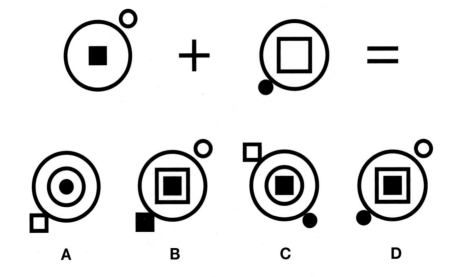

A   B   C   D

5. Which is the odd man out?

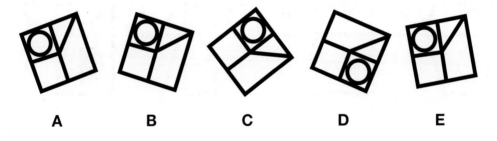

A   B   C   D   E

6. Which is the missing circle?

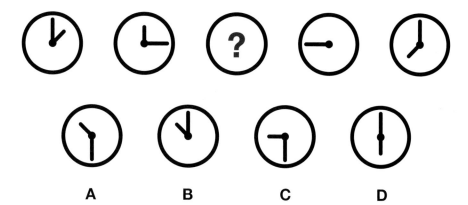

A   B   C   D

7. Which is the missing piece of the puzzle?

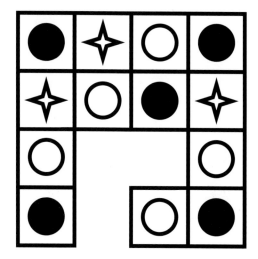

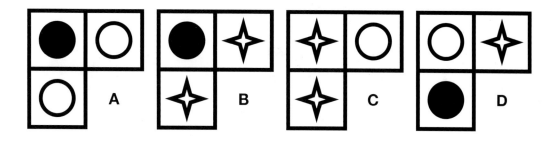

A   B   C   D

8. Which 2 figures show the same pattern?

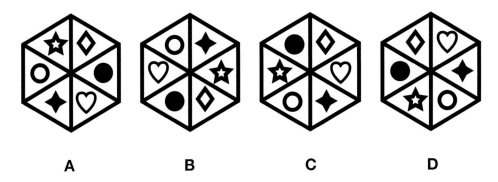

A   B   C   D

9. Select the response from items A–D that correctly replaces the "?" in the equation.

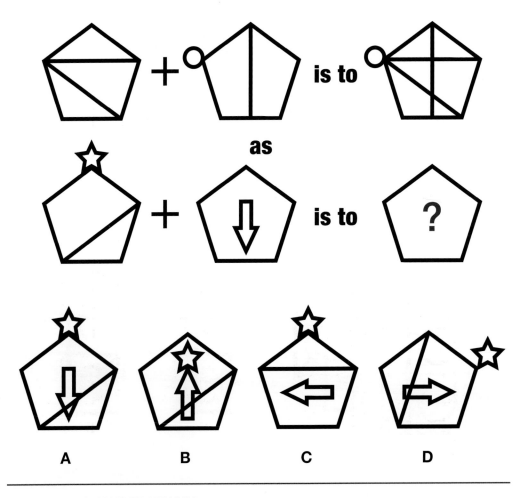

A   B   C   D

10.

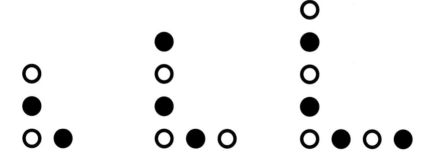

What comes next?

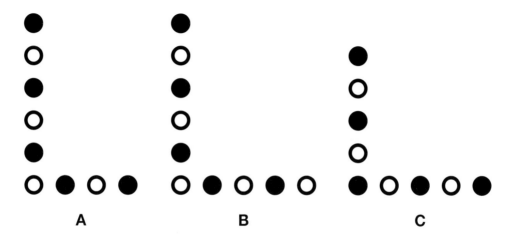

       A   B   C

11. Which is the missing tile?

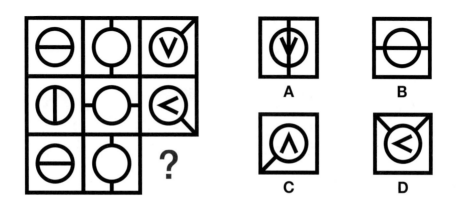

12. What should be in the circle in place of **X** ?

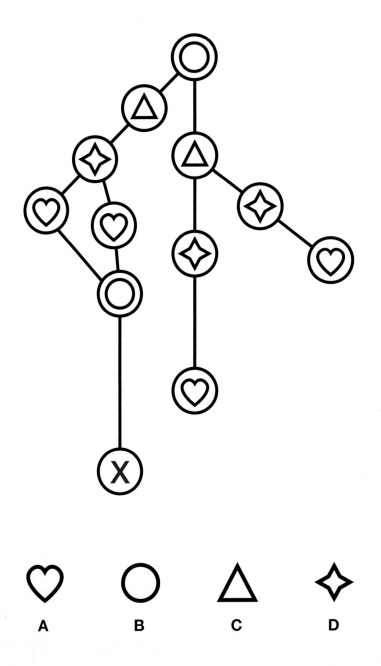

A   B   C   D

13. How many four-sided figures are in the example below?

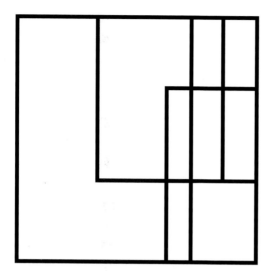

A. 6
B. 8
C. 10
D. more than 12

14. Which line, A, B, C, or D, stands at an angle closest to that of the red line?

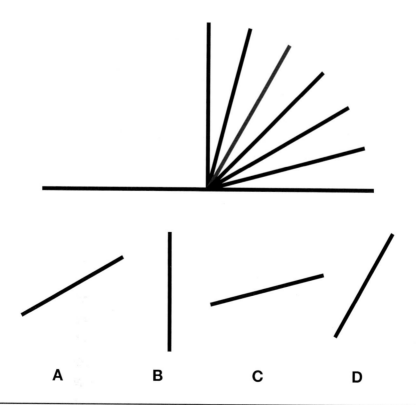

A   B   C   D

15. When this drawing is folded into a cube, which figure from selections A–D can be formed?

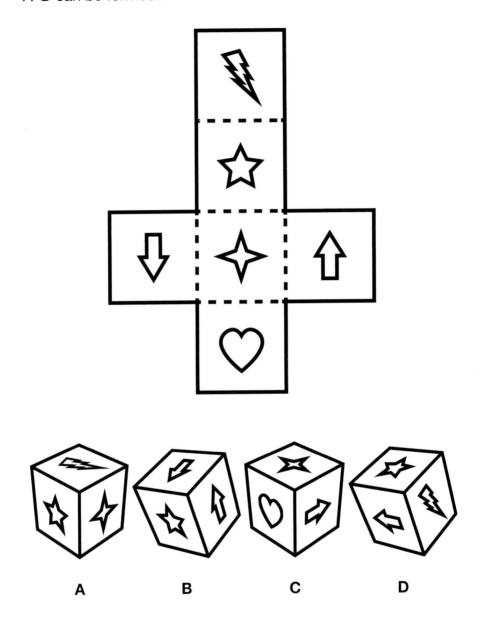

A   B   C   D

16. When this figure is folded on the dotted line, which figure from selections A–D is formed?

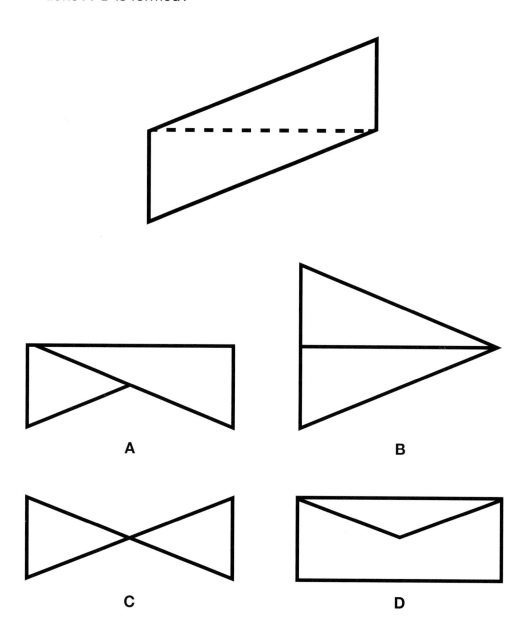

A

B

C

D

17. Reposition 2 lines to form 5 squares out of the 4, as shown below. (You will have 1 line left over.)

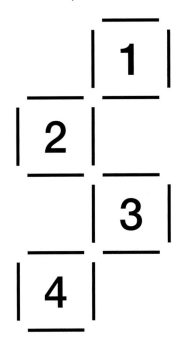

18. Select the tile that completes the equation.

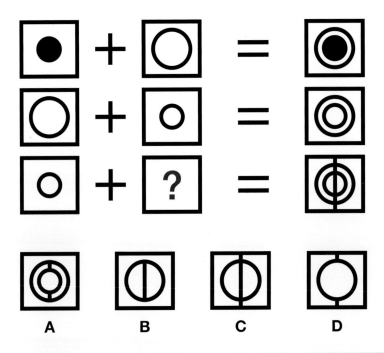

19. Select the response from items A–D that correctly replaces the **?** in the equation.

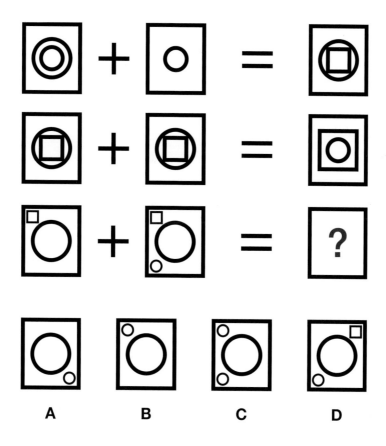

20. Of the 4 choices, which best completes the picture analogy?

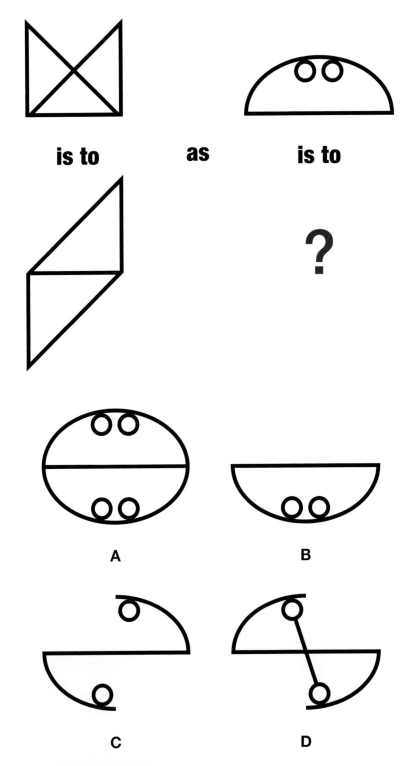

is to   as   is to

?

A

B

C

D

Answers

1. **B**

2. **C**, the oblong black dot advances up the screen, disappears, then returns from the bottom of the triangle.

3. **D**, the circle does not contain the black dot.

4. **D**

5. **D**

6. **A**, the long hand moves to the right 1/4 turn per figure; the short hand moves to the left 1/8 turn per figure.

7. **B**, starting at the upper left corner, the figures rotate black circle, star, open circle, then repeat.

8. **C** and **D**

9. **A**

10. **B**

11. **C**, each frame turns 1/4 to the right.

12. **C**, as the circles progress downward (even slanted), the pattern of circle, triangle, star, heart repeats.

13. **D**

14. **D**

15. **C**

16. **A**

17.   This   becomes this

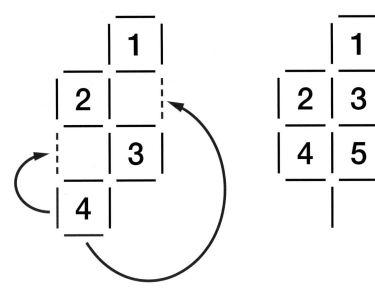

18. C

19. C, when circles are added together, they become squares and vice versa.

20. C

Reasoning

OK, put on your thinking caps. Reasoning is one of the highest executive functions that human beings possess. The progression involves taking in information, processing the data, analyzing the options based on previous experiences, and coming up with a decision that is both factual and rational.

EXAMPLES:
Here are some illustrations for practice.

1. Change the position of the words in the following passage so that the sentence makes complete sense.

   A drummer man does perhaps keep different if it is because his companions he hears not with a pace.

2. Punctuate the following text so that 3 logical sentences are formed.

   that that is is that that is not is not is not that it it is

3. The letters in the word "**OCCASION**" can easily be made into an armless figure drawing. Can you do it?

ANSWERS:
1. "If a man does not keep pace with his companions, perhaps it is because he hears a different drummer." (Henry David Thoreau, *Walden*, 1854)
2. That that is, is; that that is not, is not. Is not that it? It is.
3.

Basic

1. John shook hands with Bill. Bill shook hands with Henry. Did John shake hands with Henry?

   _____ Yes _____ No _____ Not enough information

2. I just saw a black crow. All the crows I have seen are black. Therefore, all crows are black.

   _____ Agree _____ Disagree

3. Sam is older than Rachel. Ann is older than Rachel. Sam is older than Ann. Therefore, Sam is the oldest.

   _____ Agree _____ Disagree

4. At the world archery championships, 40% of the contestants were from Europe. Half that many were from North America, and 1/20 of the total amount were from Africa. What was the percentage of contestants from continents other than Europe, North America, and Africa?

   Answer _____

5. In a herd of elephants, some are white and some are blue. Therefore, all elephants in the herd are blue or white.

   _____ Agree _____ Disagree

6. "Birds of a feather flock together" means:

   A. Most birds have feathers.
   B. Being left out of a group is lonely.
   C. All birds are arranged by flocks.
   D. Like beings seek each other's company.

7. "The apple doesn't fall far from the tree" means:

   A. All apples fall off trees.
   B. A person's traits are similar to those of others in the family.
   C. When apples fall, measure the distance.
   D. Some apples don't ever fall.

8. Fill in the blanks:

   Some _____ make things happen. Others watch

   things _____. Then there are some who don't know

   what's _____.

9. Condense the proverb "A bird in the hand is worth two in the bush" into a concise interpretation of 4 words or fewer.

   _____

10. I have 3 soccer balls. Ball A is identical to ball B; ball B is identical to ball C. Therefore, ball A and ball C are identical.

   _____ Agree   _____ Disagree

11. What word does not belong with the others?

   A. couch
   B. rug
   C. sofa
   D. chair

12. What group of letters comes next? A, AB, ABD, ABDG, ABDGK, **?**

Answer _____

13. Place the numbers 1 to 5 in the circles so that:

- the sum of the numbers 2 and 1 and all the numbers between totals 7
- the sum of the numbers 5 and 3 and all the numbers between totals 15
- the sum of the numbers 4 and 3 and all the numbers between totals 8
- the sum of the numbers 5 and 1 and all the numbers between totals 12

(Two possible answers)

◯ ◯ ◯ ◯ ◯

14. A familiar phrase has had its initial letters and word boundaries removed. What is the phrase?

IGHTOROREYES

_____

15. Which word does not belong in the group?

A. judge   **C.** plaintiff   **E.** defendant
B. jury   **D.** verdict   **F.** attorney

_____

16. Which is the odd one out? canyon, butte, ravine, gully, gorge

_____

17. Harry started at his home in Scotland and traveled first to England, then to France before heading east and taking the most direct route to the Russian border. What major bodies of water did he cross?

_____

18. What do an artist, sculptor, and novelist have in common?

_____

19. Combine 3 of the three-letter bits to produce a word that means "undetermined" or "indefinite."

ITR | CAN | ARB | MUS | ARY | CLE | WIS

_____

20. Place a word in the brackets that means the same as the words or phrases on either side of the brackets.

   [Hint: the word might be pronounced differently, depending on its meaning.]

   A. abstain [_____] chorus of a song

   B. dry sandy expanse [_____] to vacate

   C. restart [_____] summary

   D. vegetable/fruits [_____] make happen

Answers

1. Not enough information. Maybe he did, and maybe he didn't.

2. Disagree.

3. Agree.

4. 35%

5. Disagree. Some could be other colors.

6. **D**

7. **B**

8. people, happen, happening.

9. "Don't gamble"; "Don't take chances"; or "Take the sure thing" (or similar).

10. Agree. Things that are equal to the same thing are equal to each other.

11. **B**

12. **ABDGKP** (increase letters by 1-2-3, etc.)

13.

⑤ ② ④ ① ③

OR

③ ① ④ ② ⑤

14. SIGHT FOR SORE EYES

15. D

16. butte

17. The English Channel

18. All are people who produce creative works.

19. ARBITRARY

20. A. refrain
B. desert (not to be confused with "dessert," a sweet treat)
C. resume
D. produce

1. Four people in a landscape crew are working in Mr. Smith's yard. Sam is raking leaves in the front of the house. Shawn is on the east side trimming a magnolia tree. Seth is blowing the driveway on the opposite side by the garage. Stewart is in the backyard mowing the grass. Sam is on the south. If Sam switches places with Stewart, and Stewart then switches places with Seth, where is Stewart?

    A. north side
    B. south side
    C. east side
    D. west side

2. In the emergency room of a hospital, Dr. White encourages the interns to rotate with new partners at least every 4 weeks. Dr. Brown and Dr. Green have worked together 4 weeks, and Dr. Scarlet and Dr. Black have worked together 2 weeks. Dr. Scarlet does not want to work with Dr. Brown. Who should work with Dr. Green?

    A. Dr. Brown
    B. Dr. Scarlet
    C. Dr. Black
    D. Dr. White

3. Mary sat on the middle row in a football stadium that had 11 rows of bleachers. Her 2 children sat with friends; Larry sat 2 rows below his mother, and Lucy on a row higher than her mother, resting her back against her aunt Mollie's legs. Mollie sat 5 rows above her sister, Mary. List the order of the seating and the row, starting with the lowest.

    A. Mary 5, Lucy 7, Larry 3, Mollie 10
    B. Lucy 8, Larry 5, Mary 7, Mollie 9
    C. Larry 4, Mary 6, Lucy 10, Mollie 11
    D. Mary 5, Mollie 9, Larry 6, Lucy 7

4. Mo, Joe, Bo, and Flo compete in tennis. Mo has come in second place 3 times out of 7 tournaments. Joe has won 1 tournament and placed third on 2 occasions out of a total of 9 entries. Flo has had 2 second places and 1 third place out of 5 entries. Bo got entangled in the net on his first attempt, broke his ankle, and threw his racquet away. Who should be ranked as the best player?

   [Hint: assign 3 points for first place, 2 points for second place, and 1 point for third place.]

   A. Mo
   B. Joe
   C. Flo
   D. Bo

5. Today I saw a black sheep. All the other sheep I have seen are white. Therefore, all sheep are either black or white.

   _____ Yes   _____ No   _____ Not enough information

6. On vacation at the beach, Grandmother rides an adult tricycle while Grandfather enjoys inline skating on the boardwalk. My siblings and I all ride bicycles, except for baby Frances, who is in a four-wheel buggy pushed by Mother, and Fred, the next-to-youngest sibling, who is strapped in a child's seat attached to Father's bike. When my grandparents, parents, 7 siblings, and I are on an outing together, how many wheels are involved?

   A. 25
   B. 30
   C. 19
   D. 29

7. The proverb "A rolling stone gathers no moss" means: (two answers are correct).

    A. You won't develop roots if you keep on moving.
    B. Moss is good to gather.
    C. Keeping active keeps problems at bay.
    D. Stones can roll with or without moss.

8. In my hometown, the supermarket is on the northeast corner of the town square surrounding the courthouse. The barber shop is on the southeast corner. The furniture store is in the middle of a block, facing southward toward the courthouse. In what directions must I walk from the barbershop to the supermarket to avoid passing in front of the furniture store?

    A. east, then north
    B. west, then north
    C. north, then west
    D. west, then south

9. For each grouping, pick out the "on the map" name that does not belong in the list:

    A. Maine, North Carolina, Oregon, Florida, Maryland

    B. Pacific, Indian, Mediterranean, Atlantic, Arctic

    C. Denver, Houston, Philadelphia, Seattle, New Orleans

    D. Baikal, Powell, Travis, Tahoe, Mead

    E. Poland, Italy, China, Siberia, Chad

10. Statement 1: Water is valuable.
    Statement 2: Water is readily available.
    Statement 3: Things that are scarce are valuable.

    If statements 1 and 2 are correct, then statement 3 is:

    _____ True _____ False _____ Unrelated

11. Place the numbers 2, 4, 6, 8, and 10 in the circles such that:

    • the sum of 4 and 6 and all numbers between equals 18
    • the sum of 10 and 8 and all numbers between equals 24
    • the sum of 6 and 2 and all numbers between equals 20

    (Two possible answers)

    ◯ ◯ ◯ ◯ ◯

12. Restate the proverb "A hot coal burns; a cold one blackens" in a concise form of 5 words or fewer.

    _____

    _____

13. The temperature today was higher than Sunday's. Wednesday has storms predicted with the coolest weather for the week. Tuesday and Thursday are forecasted to be very warm with identical temperatures, but shy of last Friday's, which set a heat record for this time of year. Last Saturday's temperature was right in the middle of all the daily temperatures. List the days of the week (Friday through Thursday) in ascending order of daily temperatures if both the observations and predictions are correct.

_____

_____

14. A fruit basket contains more oranges than apples and more lemons than limes. The apples outnumber the limes, and the lemons out-number the oranges. The number of bananas is greater than lemons, and cherries are fewer than limes. List the fruit in descending order of quantity.

_____

_____

15. I have a friend named Ralph Jones who has big feet. His feet are so big that he has to put his pants on over his head. How can he do that?

   A. Because his feet are really big.
   B. He slides his pants down and sticks his arms out through the leg holes.
   C. That's impossible.
   D. He has learned how through practice, trial, and error.

16. Fill in the parentheses with the correct homonyms as in the example.

vegetable (_____*carrot*_____ / _____*karat*_____) weight of precious stone

A. particle (_____ / _____) harmony

B. "over yonder" (_____ / _____) possessive plural pronoun

C. one who inherits (_____ / _____) stuff we breathe

D. bone in upper arm (_____ / _____) funny

17. The following is a common phrase with the first letter of each word and the spacing removed. What is the saying?

ACKFLLRADESASTERFONE

_____

_____

18. What are the common proverbs referred to below?

    A. Flawed outcome can result from a proclivity to celerity.

    _____

    B. Prudent action may forestall repetitious endeavors.

    _____

    C. A _homo sapien_'s quintessential comrade is _canis lupus familiaris_.

    _____

19. Fill in the **?**

BRAIN : AMNESIA as ARM : ?

A. fracture   **B.** paralysis   **C.** wound

NOVEL : PUBLISHER as MOVIE : ?

A. producer   **B.** actor   **C.** director

CONTEMPLATE : MEDITATE as CONTRIVE : ?

A. devise   **B.** implement   **C.** strategy

20. Draw 4 lines that will connect all the dots without lifting your pen or retracing.

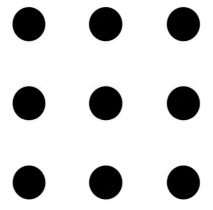

Answers

1. **D**

2. **B**

3. **C**

4. **C**

5. Inconclusive

6. **D**

7. **A**, **C**

8. **B**

9. **A.** Oregon (on the west coast; others are on the east)
    B. Mediterranean (is a sea; the others are oceans)
    C. Two answers are possible:
       Seattle (west of Continental Divide; the others are east) or
       Denver (only state capital city on the list)
    D. Baikal (is in Russia; the others are US lakes)
    E. Siberia (is a region; the rest are countries)

10. Unrelated

11.

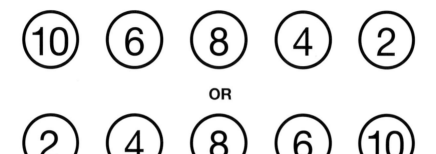

12. Extremes are dangerous (or similar interpretation).

13. Wednesday, Sunday, Monday, Saturday, Tuesday/Thursday, Friday

14. bananas, lemons, oranges, apples, limes, cherries

15. **C**

16. **A.** piece/peace
    B. there/their
    C. heir/air
    D. humerus, humorous

17. Jack of all trades, master of none

18. **A.** Haste makes waste.
    B. A stitch in time saves nine.
    C. A man's best friend is his dog.

19. **B, A, A**

20.

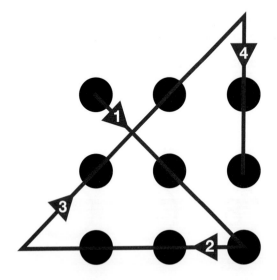

Category 11

Memory

To successfully complete this category, you will need 2 props: a *Simon* (or similar electronic game that involves both visual and auditory memory) and a friend or family member to read aloud from texts presented in this book about esoteric subjects. You will probably find the readings to be boring. That's precisely the point—to improve your listening and retention skills, even when the material may not be on a subject that holds your interest. After each reading, it is imperative that you allow a minimum of 20 minutes to lapse before answering the questions. During the wait time, occupy your mind by completing some, or all, of the additional memory exercises, including *Simon*, that are listed after the first reading.

EXAMPLE:
First, a visual pre-training assignment:

On the next page, you will see a list of 15 items in a precise order. You will have 10–15 seconds to view the page before closing the book and reproducing the entire list of 15 items in the correct order from memory. Ready? Get set. Go!

A B C

1 2 3

a b c

| || |||

○ □ △

I. **READING #1**

Listen as a friend reads the following selection. You may follow along, if you desire. Then wait at least 20 minutes, devoting your energy toward other memory exercises listed in items A–D before answering questions 1–10 based on the text.

Legends about the First US President

"Facts and Myths about George Washington" (Star 92.7's website)

George Washington was the first president of the United States and is often referred to as the "father of his country." There are several tales about this revered political figure that are not necessarily based on fact.

Did George Washington have wooden teeth?
He had false teeth, but they were not made of wood. As a matter of fact, the materials used in his false teeth were probably more uncomfortable than wood. In one set of teeth, his dentist, Dr. John Greenwood, used a cow's tooth, hippopotamus ivory, metal, and springs. They fit poorly and distorted the shape of his mouth.

Did George Washington chop down a cherry tree?
Probably not. The story was invented by a minister who wrote a biography of George Washington shortly after Washington's death. Since so little is known about Washington's childhood, the parson invented several stories about Washington's early life to illustrate the origins of the heroic qualities Washington exhibited as an adult. Introduced to countless schoolchildren as a moral tale in school textbooks, the parable has become a persistent part of American mythology.

Did George Washington throw a silver dollar across the Potomac River?

No. This myth is often told to demonstrate his strength. The Potomac River is over a mile wide, and even George Washington was not that good an athlete! Moreover, there were no silver dollars when Washington was a young man. His step-grandson, George Washington Parke Custis, reported in his memoirs that Washington once threw a piece of slate "about the size and shape of a dollar" across the Rappahannock River near Fredericksburg, Virginia. The Rappahannock River at the site of the Washington family homestead, Mount Vernon, today measures only 250 feet across, a substantial, but perhaps not impossible, distance to throw.

Did George Washington wear a wig?

No. Although wigs were fashionable, Washington kept his own hair, which he wore long and tied back in a queue, or ponytail. He did, however, powder his hair as was the custom of the time.

Is George Washington buried under the US Capitol?

No, although Congress built a vault under the Capitol building for this purpose. In his will, Washington specified that he wished to be buried at his home at Mount Vernon and that a new tomb should be constructed. His heirs honored his wish, and the vault at the US Capitol remains empty to this day.

Did George Washington live in the White House?

No. George Washington was the only president who did not live in the White House, which was not completed until after his death. During his two terms as president, the capital of the United States was located first in New York and then in Philadelphia. Washington played a large role, however, in the development of Washington, D.C., which is named after him. He was also instrumental in overseeing the design of both the Capitol Building and the White House.

Did George Washington have children?

No. George Washington had no children of his own. Washington married a wealthy widow, Martha Dandridge Custis, in 1759. She had two children from her first marriage—a son, John (nicknamed Jacky), and a daughter, Martha (nicknamed Patsy). George Washington never formally adopted these children, but he loved them and raised them as his own. So, if anyone ever says they are a direct descendant of George Washington, they are mistaken!

End of reading. Next, engage in additional memory exercises A–D for at least 20 minutes before answering questions based on this reading.

Additional Memory Exercises

A. Play several rounds of the electronic memory game *Simon.*

B. Have a friend call out numbers 1–10 at random, starting with a string of 3 numbers. You then repeat the numbers back. Increase by one number each round until you have maxed out. Most people can usually remember about 8 to 10 numbers.

C. Repeat the above exercise, but repeat the numbers back in order from largest to smallest.

D. Have a friend make a list of unrelated words and call them out for you to repeat from memory, starting with 3 items (example: apple, brown, honesty). Increase by one word each round until you've reached your limit. Highest range is typically 10 to 12 words.

II. READING #2

After listening to a reading of the text, complete additional memory exercises A–D for at least 20 minutes before answering questions 11–20.

Petit Jean

"Petit Jean State Park" (Wikipedia)

Petit Jean Mountain in the Arkansas Ozarks has an intriguing history. It begins with the story of a young French nobleman, Chavet, who lived during the period of the French exploration of America. He requested permission to explore a part of the Louisiana Territory and to claim part of the land. The King of France granted approval to Chavet.

Chavet was engaged to be married to a beautiful young girl from Paris, Adrienne Dumont. When told of his plans, she asked that they be married right away so she could accompany him. Thinking of the hardship and danger on the journey, Chavet refused her request, telling her upon his return if the country was good and safe, they would be married and go to the New World.

Adrienne refused to accept his answer and disguised herself as a male. She applied to the captain of Chavet's ship for a position as a cabin boy. The girl must have been incredibly clever in her disguise, for it is said that not even Chavet recognized her. The sailors called her Petit Jean, which is French for Little John.

The Atlantic Ocean was crossed in early spring; the vessel ascended the Mississippi River to the Arkansas River, to the foot of the mountain. The Indians on the mountain came to the river, greeted Chavet, and invited the sailors to spend time on the mountain. Chavet, Petit Jean, and the sailors spent the summer atop Petit Jean Mountain until fall approached, and then they began preparations for their voyage back to France. The ship was readied and boarded the evening before departure.

That night, Petit Jean became ill with a sickness that was strange to Chavet and his sailors. It was marked with fever, convulsions, delirium, and finally coma. Her condition was so serious at daylight that the departure was delayed. During the illness, Petit Jean's identity was discovered.

The girl confessed her deception to Chavet and begged his forgiveness. She requested that if she died, she be carried back to the mountaintop where she spent her last days and be buried at a spot overlooking the river below. The Indians made a stretcher out of deerskins and bore her up the mountain. At sundown, she died. Her gravesite on top of Petit Jean Mountain is still visited today by sightseers to this beautiful area.

Wait at least 20 minutes before answering questions based on this text.

QUESTIONS BASED ON READING #1

Legends about the First US President

1. George Washington was referred to as the _____ of his country.

    A. uncle
    B. patron saint
    C. father
    D. brother

2. His false teeth were made out of

    A. wood
    B. cement
    C. ivory and metal
    D. enamel

3. His wig was made out of

    A. human hair
    B. horse's mane
    C. animal fur
    D. didn't wear a wig

4. He probably really didn't chop down a _____ tree.

   A. pecan
   B. cherry
   C. apple
   D. maple

5. The item some people said he threw across the Potomac River was a

   A. silver dollar
   B. gold coin
   C. golf ball
   D. rock

6. The person buried in the vault under the US Capitol is:

   A. George Washington
   B. John Adams
   C. Benjamin Franklin
   D. no one

7. Washington's home is named

   A. Tara
   B. Monticello
   C. Mount Vernon
   D. Mount Olive

8. The first US capital was located in

   A. Baltimore
   B. New York
   C. Philadelphia
   D. Washington, D.C.

9. What was the first name of Washington's wife?

    A. Martha
    B. Eleanor
    C. Hillary
    D. Mamie

10. Washington's children were:

    A. a boy and girl
    B. two boys
    C. two girls
    D. he didn't have children

QUESTIONS BASED ON READING #2

Petit Jean

11. Petit Jean Mountain is located in the

    A. Ozarks
    B. Rockies
    C. Catskills
    D. Smokies

12. The state in the story is

    A. Kentucky
    B. Alaska
    C. Arkansas
    D. Tennessee

13. Chavet, the nobleman in the story, was granted permission to travel to America by the

    A. Pope
    B. Queen of Spain
    C. King of England
    D. King of France

14. Adrienne disguised herself as a

    A. sailor
    B. cabin boy
    C. cook
    D. deckhand

15. Petit Jean means

    A. big mama
    B. pretty girl
    C. Little John
    D. Little Joan

16. The bodies of water the ship had to navigate were:

    A. the Pacific Ocean, the Ohio River, and Buffalo Bayou
    B. the Indian Ocean, the Mississippi and Nile Rivers
    C. the Atlantic Ocean, the Mississippi and Arkansas Rivers
    D. the Caribbean, the Colorado and Neches Rivers

17. The illness Petit Jean developed was

    A. measles
    B. strange and fatal
    C. pneumonia
    D. appendicitis

18. Petit Jean was buried

    A. on the mountaintop
    B. in the valley
    C. in her native country
    D. near the river

19. Before she died, she was carried by

    A. sailors
    B. a ship's captain
    C. Chavet
    D. Indians

20. The stretcher was made of

    A. tree limbs
    B. poles
    C. deerskins
    D. vines

Answers

READING #1

1. C
2. C
3. D
4. B
5. A
6. D
7. C
8. B
9. A
10. D

READING #2

11. A
12. C
13. D
14. B
15. C
16. C
17. B
18. A
19. D
20. C

I.   READING #3

Ancient Theater

"Theatre of Ancient Greece" (Wikipedia)

The theater of Ancient Greece evolved from religious rites that date back to at least 1200 BC. At that time, Greece was peopled by tribes that modern people might label primitive, though the products of their creative genius still survive. In northern Greece, a cult arose that worshipped Dionysus, the god of fertility and procreation. This Cult of Dionysus, which probably originated in Asia Minor, practiced ritual celebrations that may have included alcoholic intoxication, orgies, human and animal sacrifices, and outbursts of hysteria.

The cult's most controversial practice involved uninhibited dancing and emotional displays that created an altered mental state. This altered state was known as "ecstasis," from which the word "ecstasy" is derived. The words "hysteria" and "catharsis" also derive from Greek words for emotional release or purification. Ecstasy was an important religious concept to the Greeks, who would come to see theater as a way of releasing powerful emotions through its ritual power. Though it was met with resistance, the cult spread south through the tribes of Greece over the ensuing six centuries. During this time, the rites of Dionysus became mainstream and more formalized and symbolic. The death of a tragic hero was offered up to the god rather than the sacrifice of an animal. By 600 BC these ceremonies were practiced in spring throughout much of Greece.

Essential parts of the rites of Dionysus were the chorus and an altar. The chorus, composed of forty men, functioned as one character. They would chant a hymn, accompanied by mimic gestures and music. The production was like a hymn in the middle of a mass describing the adventures of Dionysus. It was more than a play; it was a religious experience. In its earliest form it was led by a priestly main actor, who was the only other character in the play. He was followed by the chorus as a band of revelers, dancing around the altar. The actors were probably dressed as satyrs—mythological half-human, half-goat servants of Dionysus. They played drums, lyres, and flutes, and they chanted as they danced around an effigy of Dionysus. The production was given a regular form and raised to the rank of artistic poetry in about 600 BC. Introduced into

Athens shortly before 500 BC, the ritual was soon recognized as one of the competitive subjects at the various Athenian festivals. For more than a generation after its introduction, this type of production attracted the most famous poets of the day. By this time, however, it had ceased to concern itself exclusively with the adventures of Dionysus and began to depict subjects from all periods of Greek mythology. In this way, over time the ritual would evolve into stories in a "play" form called drama.

Stop and play the additional memory games previously listed for at least 20 minutes before answering questions 1–15.

II.   READING #4

The Great Belize Blue Hole

Adapted from Belize Tourist website

The Great Belize Blue Hole is a world-class destination in the Caribbean for recreational scuba divers attracted by the opportunity to dive in crystal-clear waters and see myriad of species of marine life, including tropical fish and spectacular coral formations. This large underwater sinkhole off the coast of Belize can be approached from the country's most popular and largest island, Ambergris Caye, famous for its beaches, laid-back lifestyle, fishing, snorkeling, and clear turquoise waters. The Blue Hole lies near the center of Lighthouse Reef, a small atoll sixty miles from the mainland and Belize City, the nation's capital.

Belize is on the northeastern coast of Central America, surrounded by Mexico on the north and Guatemala on the south and west. The country was formerly known as British Honduras and was officially renamed Belize in 1973. It is the only nation in Central America with English as its official language. Ruins of the ancient Mayan civilization are found on the mainland.

The Blue Hole is circular in shape, over 984 feet across and 410 feet deep. Labeled the world's largest natural formation of its kind, it can be identified in satellite photographs from space. The Great Blue Hole is part of the larger Barrier Reef Reserve System, a World Heritage Site of the United Nations Organization for Education, Science and Culture (UNESCO).

This site was made famous by Jacques Cousteau, who declared it one of the top ten scuba diving sites in the world. In 1971, he brought his ship, the *Calypso*, to the hole to chart its depths. In 2012, the Discovery Channel ranked the Great Blue Hole as number one on its list of "The 10 Most Amazing Places on Earth."

Stop and play *Simon* or other memory games for 20 minutes before answering questions 16–25.

QUESTIONS BASED ON READING #3

Ancient Theater

1. The country of reference in the reading was

    A. Egypt
    B. Italy
    C. Turkey
    D. Greece

2. The early tribes could best be described as (more than one correct answer)

    A. primitive
    B. creative genius
    C. uneducated
    D. drunkards

3. The god that was worshipped was called

    A. Athena
    B. Dionysius
    C. Diana
    D. Hermes

4. New words from this era are

    A. altar, worship, chant
    B. hysteria, chorus, satyr
    C. hysteria, ecstasy, catharsis
    D. chorus, catharsis, ritual

5. The origin of theater probably started in

    A. the Jurassic period
    B. 1200 AD
    C. 1200 BC
    D. 100 AD

6. The time of year the ceremonies were practiced was

    A. fall
    B. winter
    C. spring
    D. summer

7. Essential parts were

    A. fife and drum
    B. song and dance
    C. chorus and altar
    D. food and drink

8. The ceremony was more than a play; it was a(n) _____ experience.

    A. embarrassing
    B. religious
    C. humbling
    D. offensive

9. The number of characters in a production was

    A. 40
    B. 41
    C. 2
    D. 600

10. The main character was

    A. priest-like
    B. princely
    C. roguish
    D. hawk-like

11. The actors were likely dressed as

    A. angels
    B. Satan
    C. satyrs
    D. traders

12. Instruments used were

    A. drums, lyres, and flutes
    B. horns, cymbals, and lutes
    C. drums, bells, and harps
    D. tambourines, reeds, and pipes

13. This type of production attracted the most important _____ of that day.

    A. writers
    B. poets
    C. orators
    D. musicians

14. Later plays were based on

    A. military figures
    B. mythology figures
    C. local leaders
    D. tribal customs

15. The stories evolved into plays called

    A. tragedy
    B. comedy
    C. drama
    D. satire

QUESTIONS BASED ON READING #4

The Great Belize Blue Hole

16. Near what country is the Blue Hole located?

    A. Honduras
    B. Guatemala
    C. Mexico
    D. Belize

17. What body of water contains the Blue Hole?

    A. the Indian Ocean
    B. the Caribbean
    C. the Mediterranean
    D. the Atlantic Ocean

18. The largest island of the country is called

    A. Puerto Rico
    B. Ambergris Caye
    C. Lighthouse Island
    D. Blue Reef

19. The main activity at the Blue Hole is

    A. swimming
    B. scuba diving
    C. fishing
    D. boating

20. The official language of the country in the reading is

    A. Spanish
    B. English
    C. Portuguese
    D. Creole

21. The Blue Hole's shape is

    A. circular
    B. triangular
    C. rectangular
    D. oval

22. An ancient civilization on the country's mainland was

    A. Aztec
    B. Indian
    C. Mayan
    D. Incan

23. A famous underwater explorer/photographer who measured the depth of the Blue Hole is

    A. Marco Polo
    B. Jacques Cousteau
    C. Christopher Columbus
    D. DeSoto

24. His boat was named the

    A. *African Queen*
    B. *Bounty*
    C. *Santa Marie*
    D. *Calypso*

25. The Blue Hole was named as the most amazing place on earth by

    A. National Geographic
    B. Google
    C. Discovery Channel
    D. Disney Channel

Answers

READING #3

1. D

2. B or C

3. B

4. C

5. C

6. C

7. C

8. B

9. C

10. A

11. C

12. A

13. B

14. B

15. C

READING #4

16. D

17. B

18. B

19. B

20. B

21. A

22. C

23. B

24. D

25. C

Category 12

Speed Training

TARGETED SKILLS: speed and concentration.

The exercises in this unit provide practice in gathering and processing information quickly and making decisions more quickly based on the given information. It's important to stretch these cognitive muscles to maintain mental sharpness as we age. These exercises involve completing a variety of timed activities. Practice repeated times by first making copies from the originals in this manual.

EXAMPLE:

There are 7 traditional colors in the rainbow in a unique order. You have 30 seconds to draw a line from the colors listed below to the correct arch.

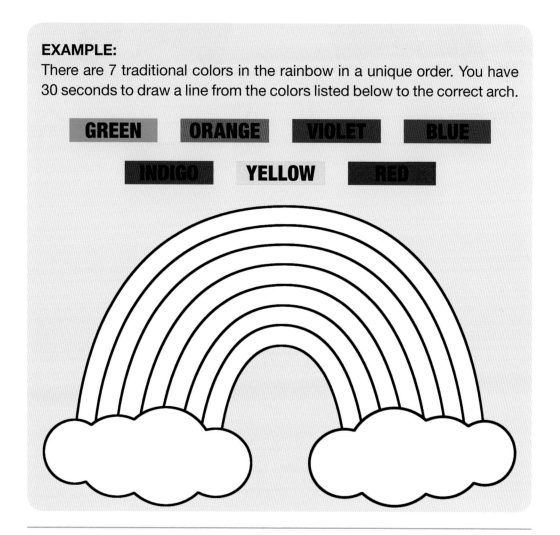

ANSWER:
The colors of the rainbow are as follows: Red, Orange, Yellow, Green, Blue, Indigo, and Violet. An easy way of remembering this order is **ROY G. BIV**.

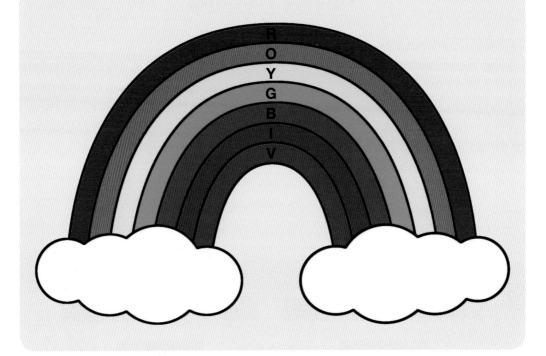

1. Draw lines that connect the cities on the map below according to alphabetical order in 6 minutes or less. The task starts with Albuquerque and ends with Washington, DC. First, set your timer. Now go!

2. List the names of 30 animals. You have 6 minutes to complete this exercise.

1. _____   16. _____

2. _____   17. _____

3. _____   18. _____

4. _____   19. _____

5. _____   20. _____

6. _____   21. _____

7. _____   22. _____

8. _____   23. _____

9. _____   24. _____

10. _____   25. _____

11. _____   26. _____

12. _____   27. _____

13. _____   28. _____

14. _____   29. _____

15. _____   30. _____

3. Complete the following serial subtractions and record your times:

    A. Subtract 3 from 20 and continue subtracting 3 until you reach 0 or a negative number.

_____

_____

Time _____

    B. Subtract 4 from 50 and continue subtracting 4 until you reach 0 or a negative number.

_____

_____

Time _____

    C. Subtract 7 from 100 and continue subtracting 7 until you reach 0 or a negative number.

_____

_____

Time _____

4. BATES ALPHABET IMAGE TRAIL

Draw a line connecting the images in alphabetical order, starting with **A**pple and ending with **Z**ebra. Make a copy for a repeat challenge and record your times. (Drawn by the grandchildren.)

Time: _____ Repeat: _____

5. List 30 fruits and vegetables in 6 minutes or less.

1. _____

2. _____

3. _____

4. _____

5. _____

6. _____

7. _____

8. _____

9. _____

10. _____

11. _____

12. _____

13. _____

14. _____

15. _____

16. _____

17. _____

18. _____

19. _____

20. _____

21. _____

22. _____

23. _____

24. _____

25. _____

26. _____

27. _____

28. _____

29. _____

30. _____

6. Connect the items in numerical order based on face value of the image. For this purpose, the following values are assigned to special cards: Ace = 1, Jack = 11, Queen = 12, King = 13. Start with the double blank domino, and you will find the numbers alternate between cards and dominoes. Before starting, make copies of the exercise to repeat your efforts and improve your speed.

7. Match anagrammed words 1–20 with the list of associated words A–T in 5 minutes or less.

1. Bare, bear   _____ A. Walk, swap

2. Option, potion   _____ B. Slant, pick up

3. Silent, listen   _____ C. Waist-shaper, take out

4. Pool, loop   _____ D. Shooters, wildebeests

5. Acres, races   _____ E. Swanky, purchase seeking

6. Related, altered   _____ F. Mute, hear

7. Dealing, aligned   _____ G. Odd, enthusiastic

8. Angle, glean   _____ H. Stay, seaworthy

9. Santa, Satan   _____ I. Equine, beach

10. Remain, marine   _____ J. Nude, grizzly

11. Tread, trade   _____ K. Land, contests

12. Sainted, stained   _____ L. Jolly elf, evil one

13. Corset, escort   _____ M. Choo-choo, storyteller

14. Introduces, reductions   _____ N. Choice, magic brew

15. Rail, liar   _____ O. Haloed, soiled

16. Regal, large   _____ P. Ride together, lap

17. Guns, gnus   _____ Q. Card toss, sided with

18. Horse, shore   _____ R. Makes acquainted, losses

19. Posh, shop   _____ S. Kinglike, big

20. Weird, wired   _____ T. Cousins, changed

8. Play the speed game *Bop It*. Record your highest level.

9. Draw lines connecting the letters of the alphabet. This is a timed exercise.

　　Write your time here:

_____ minutes _____ seconds

A　　　　Z　　　　R　　　　　　E

　　　H　　　M

　　　　　　　　　Q

L

　　　T　　F　　　　　B

D　　　　　　　S

　　　　　　Y

X　　I　　　　　　K

　　　　　C

P　　　V　　　　W　　U

　　J　　N　　　　O　　G

10. Draw lines that connect the letters to the corresponding numbers, starting with A to 1, then 1 to B, B to 2, 2 to C, etc. This is a timed exercise.

Write your time here:

_____ minutes _____ seconds

A 20 Z 12 R E

14 H M 8 15 11

L 25 Q
  2 16 21 26 B

   3 T S 4

D 1 13 F 6

X 19 I Y 10 K

  9 C W 23

P 7 V 17 U

  22

J 24 N 18 5 O G

Answers

1. Cities in correct alphabetical order

Albuquerque	Minneapolis
Atlanta	Nashville
Billings	New Orleans
Boise	New York City
Boston	Omaha
Chicago	Portland
Dallas	San Francisco
Denver	Seattle
Houston	St. Louis
Las Vegas	Washington, DC
Miami	

7.

A. 11		**K.** 5	
B. 8		**L.** 9	
C. 13		**M.** 15	
D. 17		**N.** 2	
E. 19		**O.** 12	
F. 3		**P.** 4	
G. 20		**Q.** 7	
H. 10		**R.** 14	
I. 18		**S.** 16	
J. 1		**T.** 6	

Epilogue

Congratulations. By finishing this course, you have completed over 500 exercises that targeted improving your skills in mathematics, vocabulary, word usage, reasoning, judgment, memory, concentration, speed processing, visual-spatial, picture recognition, matching, and ratios. Wow! That's quite a monumental task. I hope you can feel a "humming" of new learning circuits that will continue to enhance your mental sharpness. Keep your passion and share your accomplishments with others. Thanks for taking the journey with me.

Joe B. Bates, MD

THE END

About the Author

Dr. Joe Bates is a board-certified psychiatrist and pediatrician who currently serves as the clinical director at Rusk State Hospital in Rusk, Texas. He is a native of Homer, Louisiana, and graduated from LSU School of Medicine in New Orleans, where he was president of the Alpha Omega Alpha medical honor society and was honored with the "Highest Ideals of Medicine" award.

Dr. Bates received the Bronze Star for his service in Vietnam with the US Army as a major in the Medical Corps. He completed residencies at Baylor College of Medicine in Houston and has taken a leadership role in medical practice and teaching for the past fifty years.

In 2013, a wellness program designed by Dr. Bates was the recipient of the David Pharis award for making significant contributions to the safety and quality of inpatient care and outcomes for Texas state psychiatric hospitals. This program has recently been endorsed by the Joint Commission and is included in the national Leading Practice Library.

Dr. Bates is a member of the Christian Medical Society and has traveled to Russia, Estonia, and Belize on mission trips. He was awarded the national 2015 Mensa Intellectual Benefits to Society Award for his work with cognitive remediation training. He and his wife, Paula, live in Tyler, Texas, and are the proud parents of four children and grandparents of thirteen.